ⓑutterfly

Name_____

each picture which begins with the sound of **B**.

✕ the other pictures.

(t)urtle

Name_____

a line from each turtle to a picture which begins with the sound of T.

the T pictures.

Review:

 B b and  Tt

 the letter that stands for the beginning sound.

b   t   b   t   b   t

b   t   b   t   b   t

b   t   b   t   b   t

the pictures: b - green   t - yellow

Car

C   c

Cc under each picture which begins with the sound of C.

the C pictures.

4

Sun

Name_____

S S

a line from the sun to each picture which begins with the sound of **S**.

the **S** pictures.

5

 **Review:**

Name_____

 and

✏ the letters. 🖍 the picture which begins with the sound of the letters.

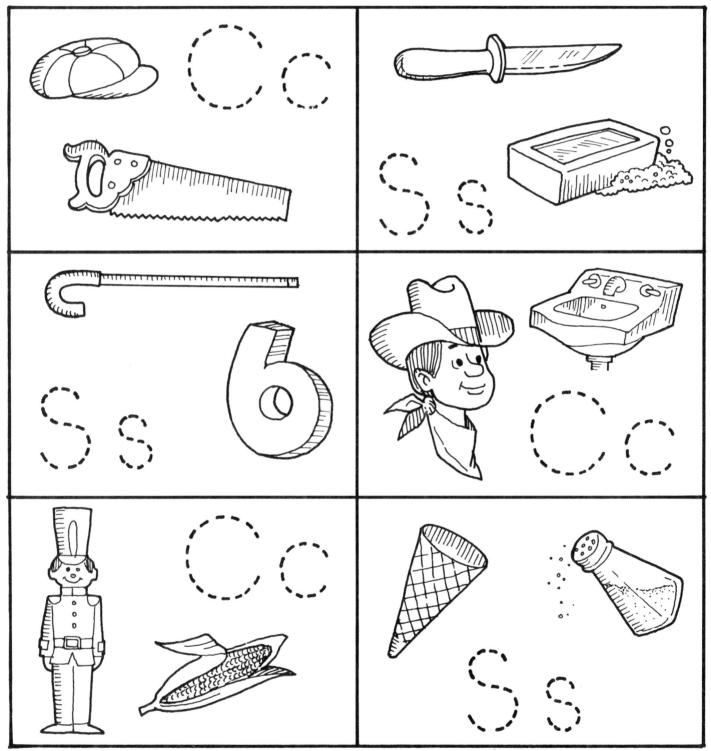

Name_____

d o g

D d

the letters. _the pictures in each row which begin with the sound of **D**._

the **D** pictures.

mushroom

Name_____

M   m

the pictures which begin with the sound of **M**.

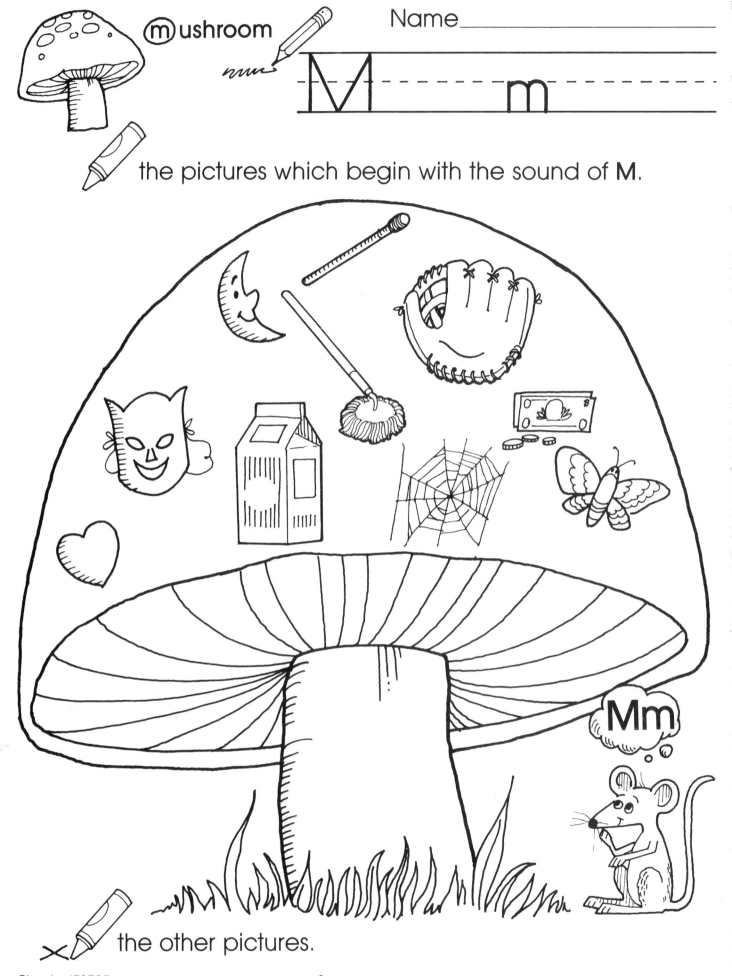

Mm

the other pictures.

Review:  Dd and  Mm

 the beginning sound of each picture.

D M   D M   D M

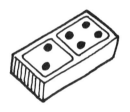

D M   D M   D M

D M   D M   D M

the pictures: D - red   M - blue

(f)ish

Name_____

F   f

each picture which begins with the sound of F.

the other pictures.

rainbow

Name_____

R - - - - - - - - r - - - - - -

a line from the **Rr** to each picture which begins with the sound of R.

Rr

the **R** pictures.

11

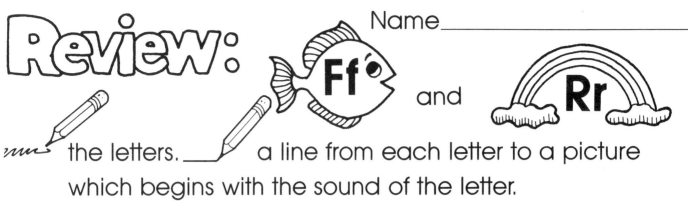

Review:

Name_____

Ff and **Rr**

✎ the letters. ✎ a line from each letter to a picture which begins with the sound of the letter.

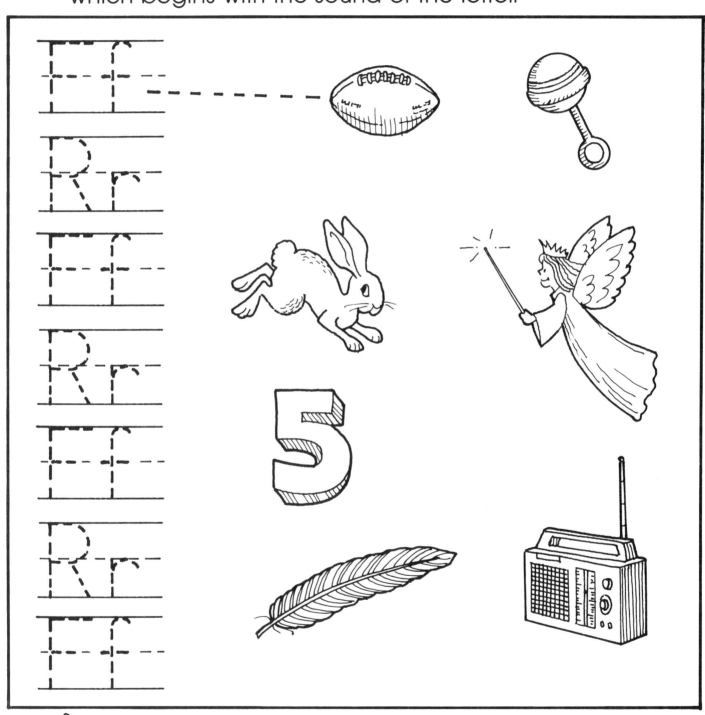

the pictures: **F** - purple **R** - green

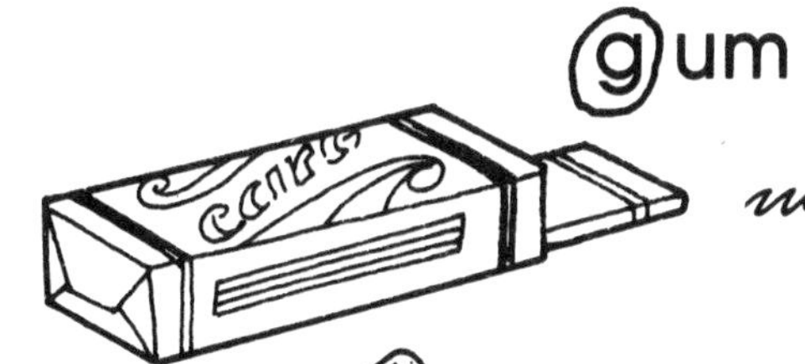

@um

G   g

Gg under each picture which begins with the sound of **G**.

the **G** pictures.

Name_____

P
P

the picture in each 🥧 that begins with the sound of P.

Ⓟie

✗ the other pictures.

Review:

Gg  and Pp

the picture which begins with the sound of each letter.

15

Web

Name_____

W   W

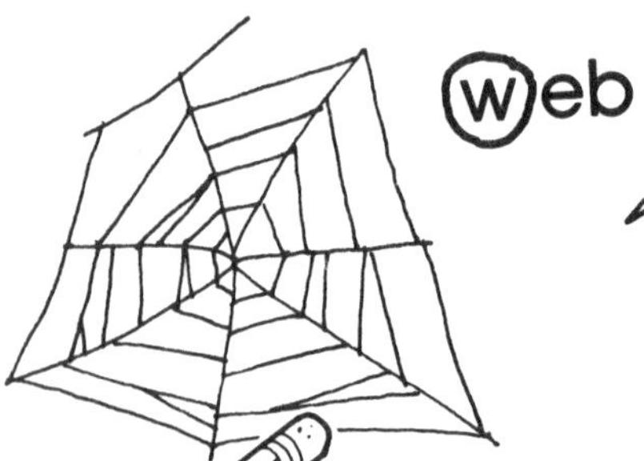

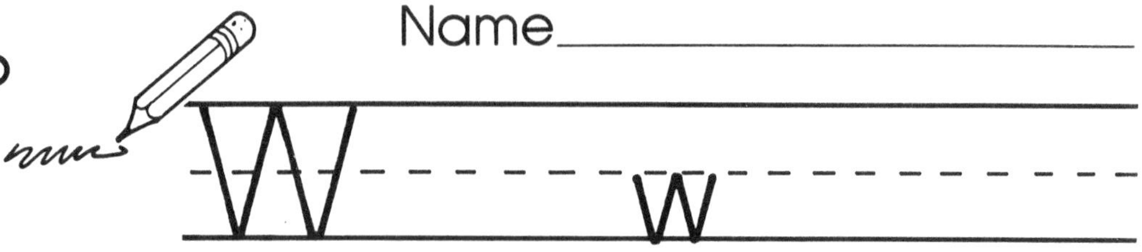

a line from the web to each picture which begins with the sound of **W**.

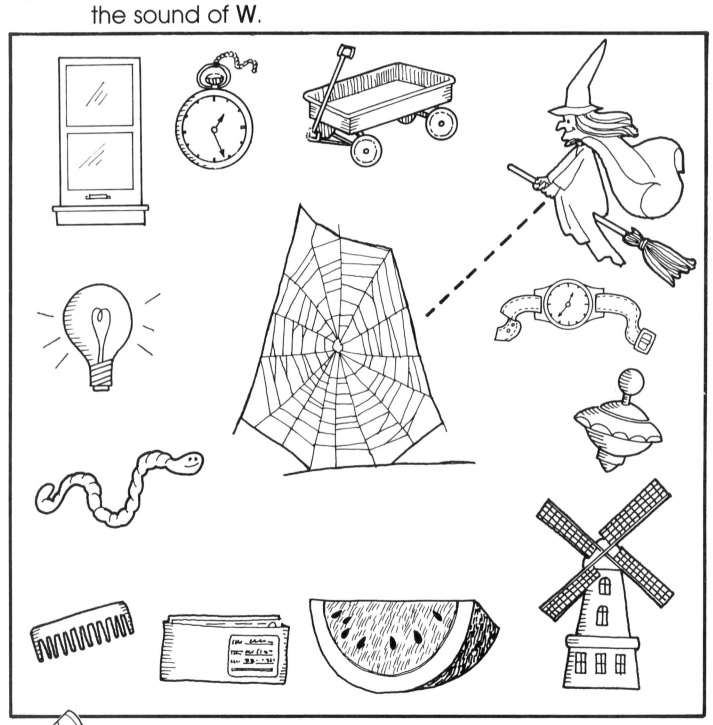

the **W** pictures.

(j)am

Name_____

J   j

____ the letters. ____ the pictures in each row which begin with the sound of J.

____ the J pictures.

Review:   Ww and

 the letter that stands for the beginning sound of each picture.

W
J

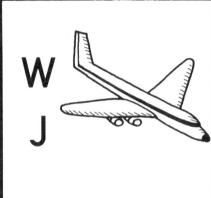

W
J

W
J

W
J

W
J

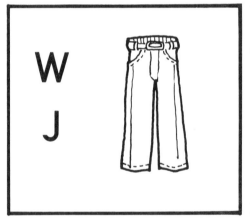

W
J

W
J

W
J

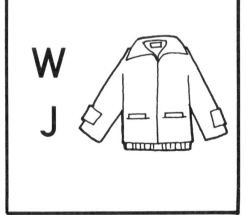

W
J

the pictures: W - yellow   J - red

(h)ouse

Name_____

H - - - - h - - - - - -

each square green if its picture begins with the sound of **H**.

the other squares yellow.

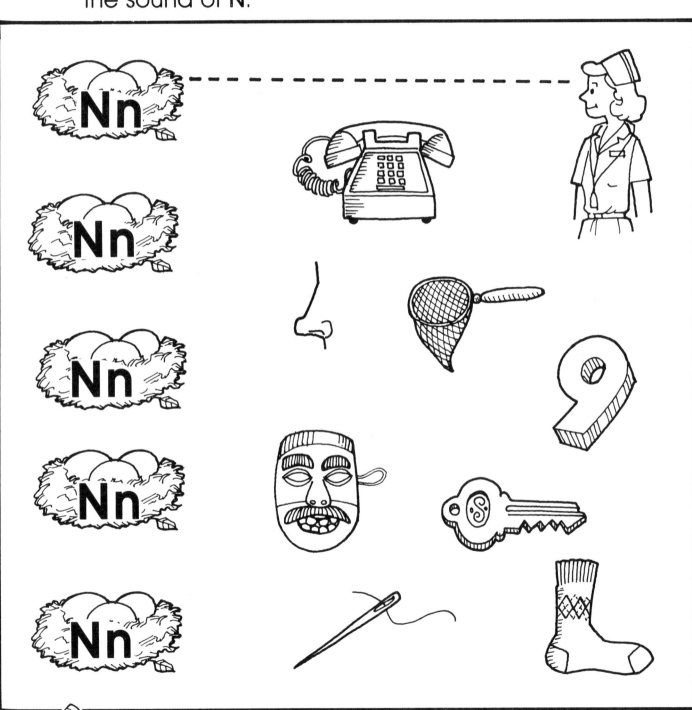

(n)est

Name_____

N   n

_____ a line from each nest to a picture which begins with the sound of **N**.

_____ the **N** pictures.

Review:

Name_____

 and

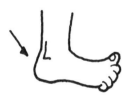 each picture the correct color for its beginning sound.

H - red N - yellow	H - orange N - blue

H - green N - purple	H - yellow N - green

H - blue N - red	H - purple N - orange

Key

Name_____

K   k

each picture which begins with the sound of K.

22

Ⓥalentine   Name_____

V   V

✏ a line from the Ⓥⅴ to each picture which begins with
the sound of V.

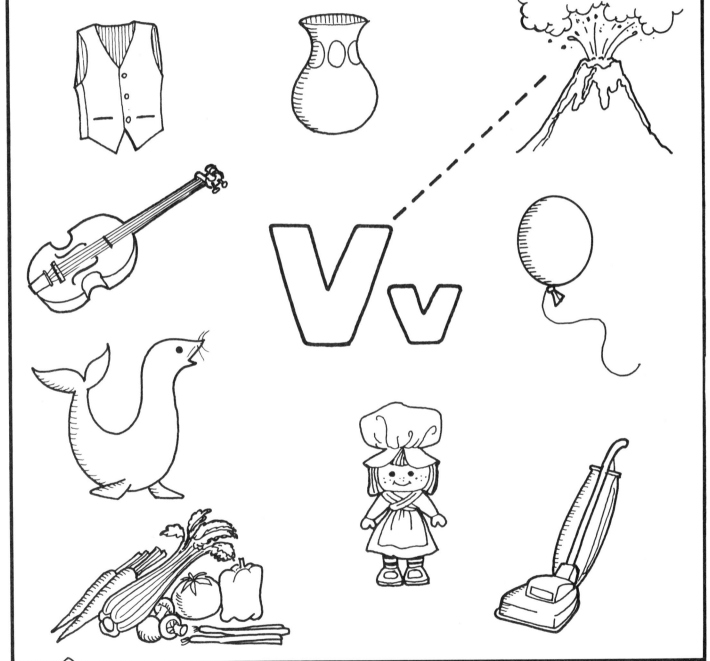

🖍 the V pictures.

Review:

Vv and **Kk**

_____ the letters. _____ a line from each letter to a picture which begins with the sound of the letter.

the pictures: K - orange   V - blue

24

Ladybug

Ll under each picture which begins with the sound of L.

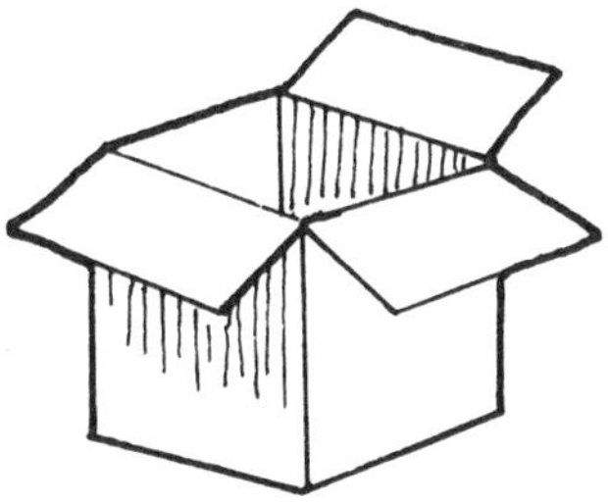

the L pictures.

25

quilt

Name_____

Q   q

each square blue if its picture begins with the sound of **Q**.

the other squares orange.

Review:

Name_____

Ll and **Qq**

✏️ the letters. 🖍️ the picture which begins with the sound of the letters.

Yo-yo

Name_____

Y y

a line from each yo-yo to a picture which begins with the sound of Y.

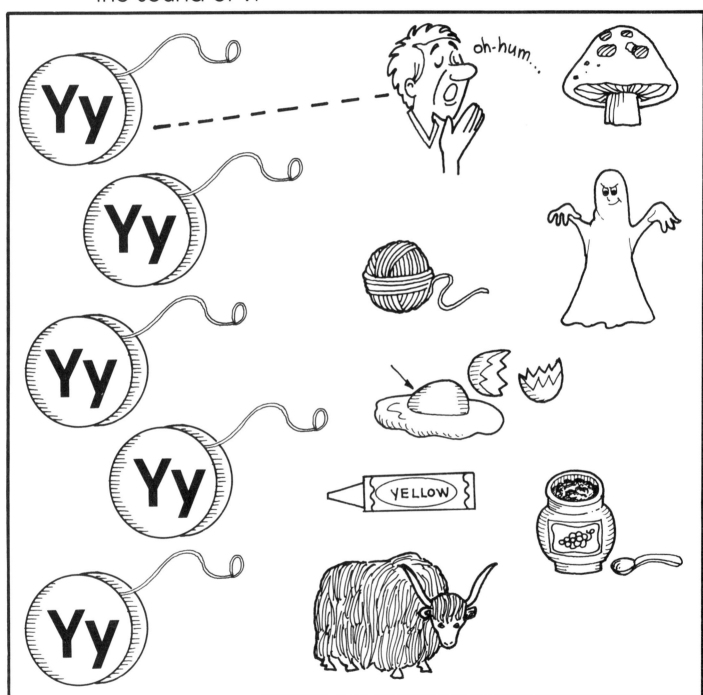

oh-hum...

YELLOW

the Y pictures.

(z)ipper

Name_____

Z

each picture which begins with the sound of Z.

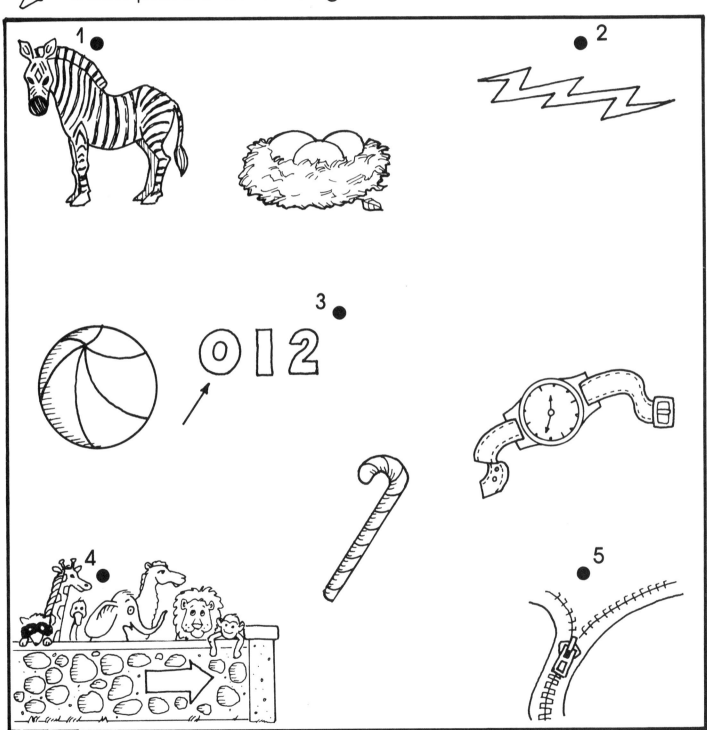

1

2

3

4

5

a line from 1-5.

Review:

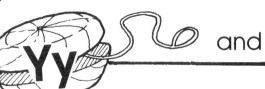 **Yy** and **Zz**

 the beginning sound of each picture.

oh-hum.

 Y   Z

 Y   Z

 Y   Z

 Y   Z

 Y   Z

 Y   Z

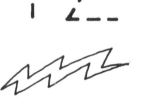

0 1 2
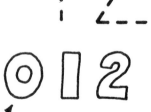

 Y   Z

 Y   Z

 Y   Z

 the pictures: **Y** - orange   **Z** - purple

Name_____

tu(b) and lea(f)

a line from each 🪣 and 🍁 to a picture which **ends** with the same sound.

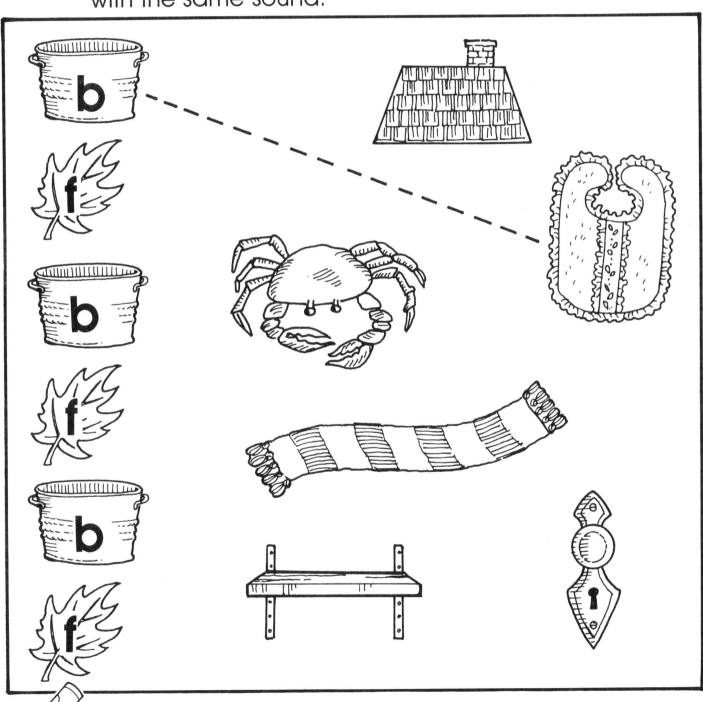

the pictures: **b** - red   **f** - yellow

 han**d**

and

 bu**g**

the shapes: **green** - ends with the sound of **D**
red - ends with the sound of **G**

moo(n) **and** ja(m)

Name_____

the letters. _____ a line from each letter to a picture which **ends** with the sound of each letter.

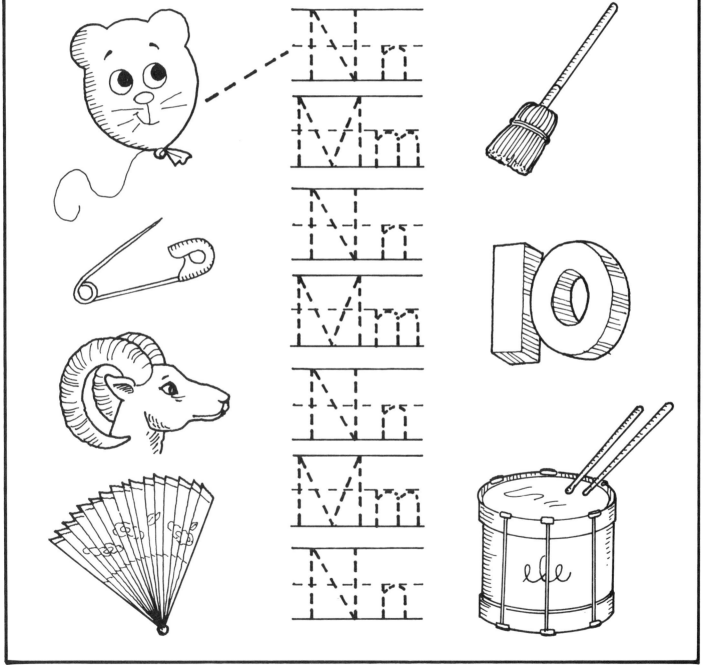

the pictures: N - orange M - purple

for k  and owl

the letter that stands for the ending sound of each picture.

k l	k l	k l
k l	k l	k l
k l	k l	k l

the pictures.

34

sta(r) *and* hear(t) *and* bo(x)

a yellow ☆ around each picture which ends with the sound of **R**.

a red ♡ around each picture which ends with the sound of **T**.

a black ⬜ around each picture which ends with the sound of **X**.

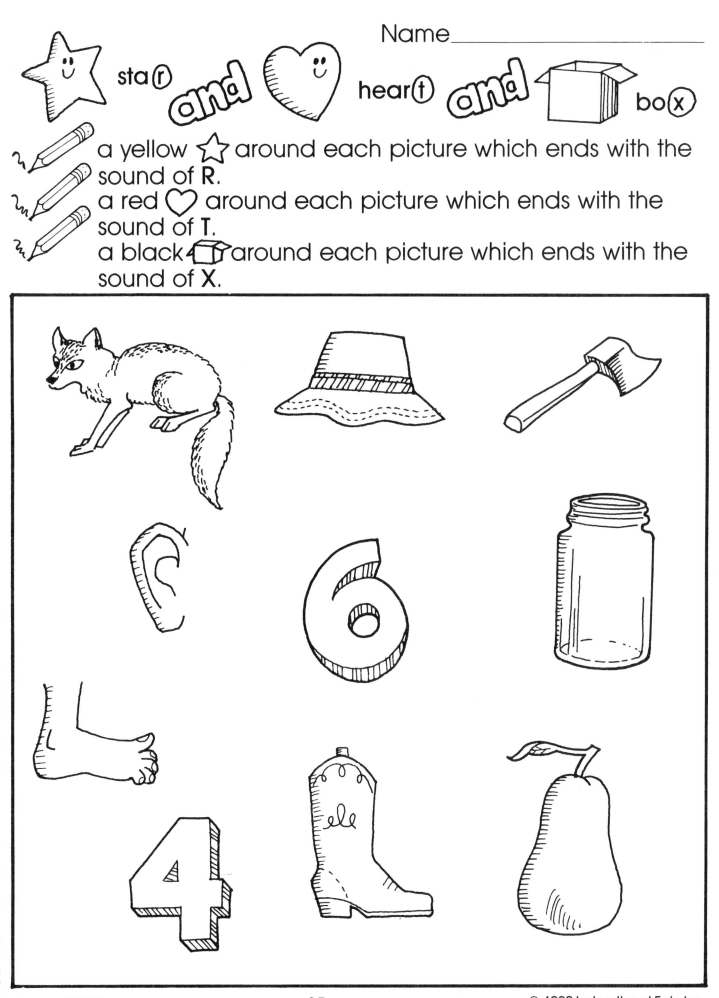

Short A

a on each line. Draw a line from each word to the correct picture.

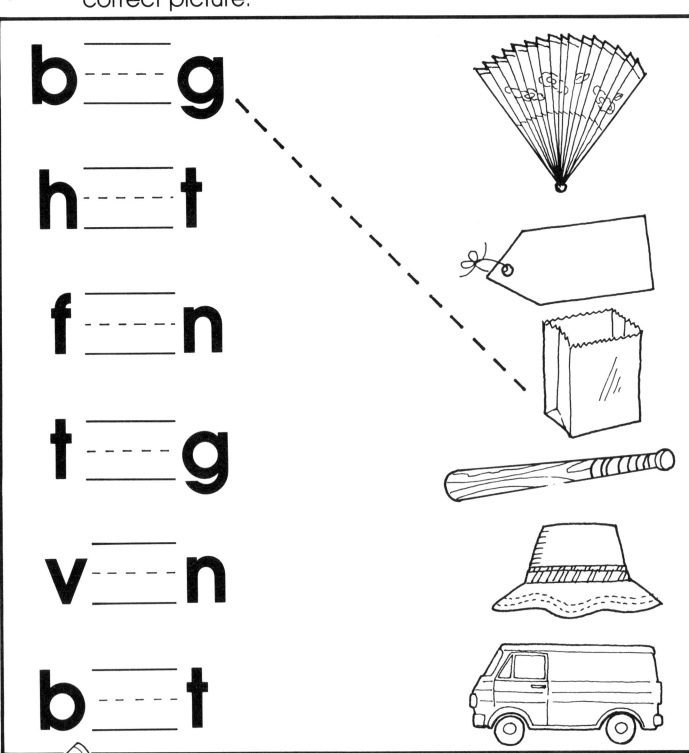

b __ g

h __ t

f __ n

t __ g

v __ n

b __ t

the pictures.

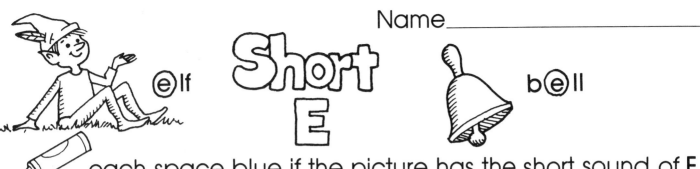

Name_____

Short E

elf   bell

each space blue if the picture has the short sound of **E**.

37

Short E

✏️ an **e** on each line. 🖍️ the correct picture for each word.

n — t

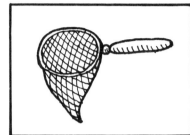 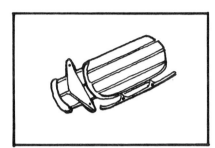

r — d

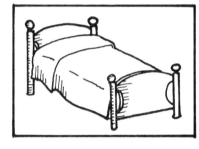 

j — t

 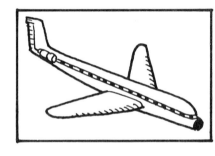

h — n

t — n

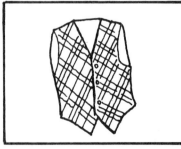 

Short E

Read each sentence. the correct words on the lines.

the words in the puzzle.

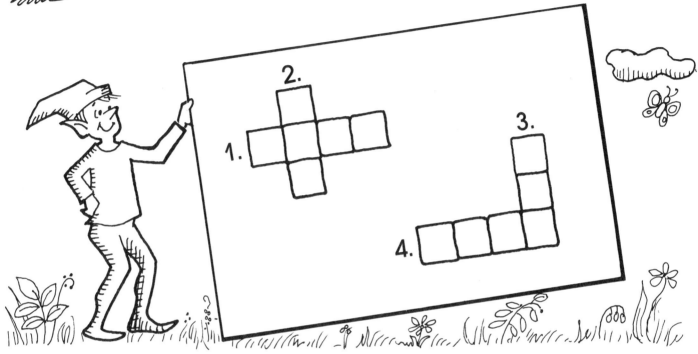

1. _____vest_____red_____

‒ ‒ ‒ ‒ ‒ ‒ ‒ ‒ ‒ ‒ ‒ ‒ ‒ ‒

I have a _____.

2. _____hen_____bed_____

‒ ‒ ‒ ‒ ‒ ‒ ‒ ‒ ‒ ‒ ‒ ‒ ‒ ‒

I am in _____.

3. _____net_____ten_____

‒ ‒ ‒ ‒ ‒ ‒ ‒ ‒ ‒ ‒ ‒ ‒ ‒ ‒

I have a _____.

4. _____pet_____tent_____

‒ ‒ ‒ ‒ ‒ ‒ ‒ ‒ ‒ ‒ ‒ ‒ ‒ ‒

I am in a _____.

Review: Short A and E

Name_____

a or e on each line to name the pictures.  each word in the puzzle.

h_ _t   n_ _t   l_ _mp

    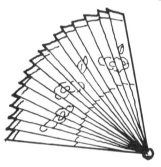

t _ _n   f _ _n

f	l	a	m	p
a	h	x	j	r
n	a	m	a	b
x	t	z	m	v
n	e	t	k	e
r	y	g	b	s
v	m	x	e	t
t	e	n	d	z

  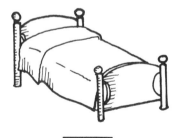

v_ _st   j_ _m   b_ _d

 the pictures: **green** - short **a**   **yellow** - short **e**

Short I

i on each line. the correct picture for each word.

p __ g 	**l __ d** 
s __ x  	**m __ lk** 
w __ g  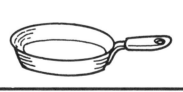	**p __ n** 
g __ ft  	**l __ ps**  

Review:  Short I

Read each sentence. ✎ the correct words on the lines.
✎ the words in the puzzle.

bib   pig
_____

I have a _____.

six   wig
_____

I have a _____.

list   pin
_____

I have a _____.

mitt   lid
_____

I have a _____.

m	o	b	i	b
i	x	r	g	s
t	l	i	s	t
t	w	i	g	v

Name_____

Short o

o on each line. ✏️ 🖍️ each sock the correct color.

d — **g**
red

m — **p**
green

t — **p**
orange

h — **t**
yellow

b — **x**
blue

d — **t**
purple

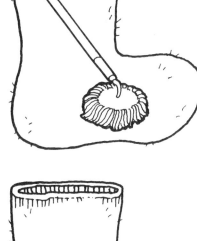

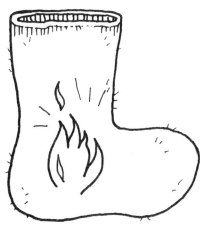

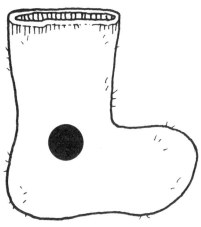

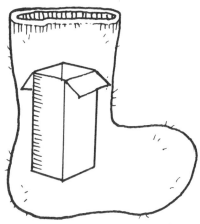

Short O

Name_____

Read each sentence. ✏ the correct word. ✏ the word on the line.

	I have a _____.	sock cot
	I have a _____.	hot doll
	I have a _____.	job mop
	I have a _____.	rod fox
	I have a _____.	dot pot

Name_____

Short U

up

d(u)ck

each space purple if the picture has the short sound of U.

the other spaces yellow.

Short U

u on each line. Draw a line from each word to the correct picture.

j __ g

c __ p

n __ t

b __ s

t __ b

r __ g

 the pictures.

46

Short U

Read each sentence. the correct ⊏⊐ to match the picture.

1. The duck has a { cup { tub .

2. The duck has a { jug { nut .

3. The duck has a { gum { bus .

4. The duck has a { bug { sun .

5. The duck has a { tub { rug .

 the pictures.

Review: Short

A E I O U

the pictures in each row with the correct vowel sound.

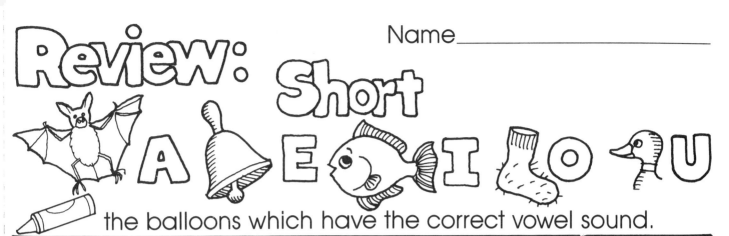

Review: Short A E I O U

the balloons which have the correct vowel sound.

Name_____

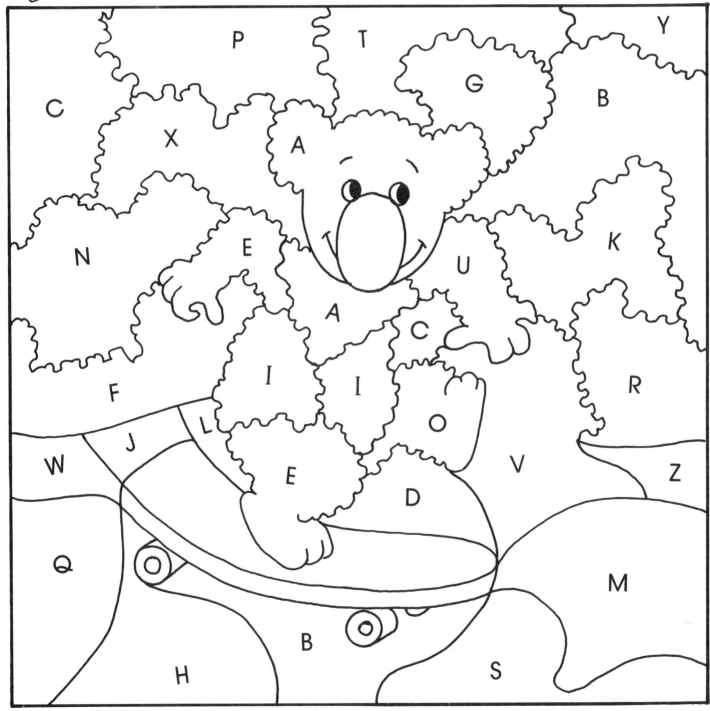

the vowel spaces red. (A E I O U)
the consonant spaces yellow.

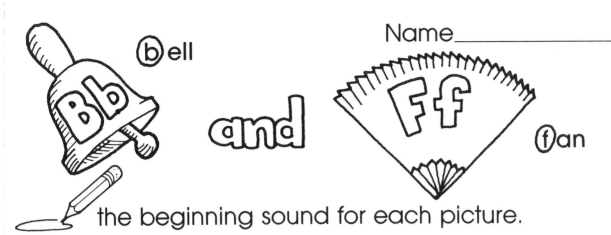

bell **and** **f**an

the beginning sound for each picture.

the pictures: **B** - green   **F** - yellow

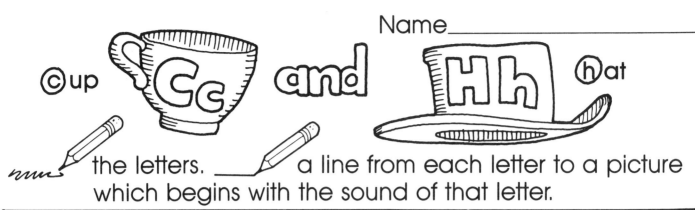

Name_____

©up **Cc** and **Hh** (h)at

_____ the letters. _____ a line from each letter to a picture which begins with the sound of that letter.

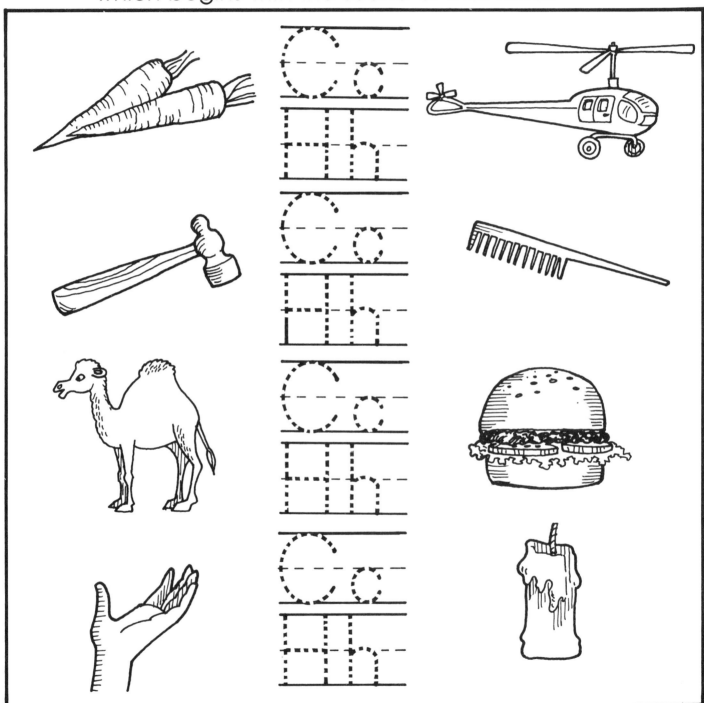

the pictures: **C** - red   **H** - purple

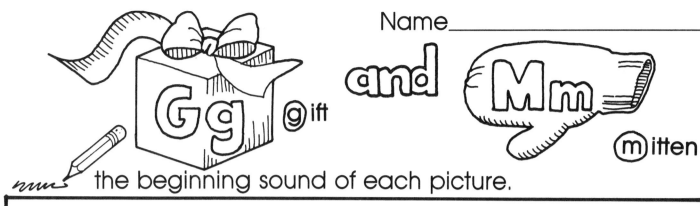

Name _____

G g gift **and** **M m**
ⓜitten

the beginning sound of each picture.

G M   G M   G M

G M   G M   G M

G M   G M   G M

the pictures: **G** - brown **M** - red

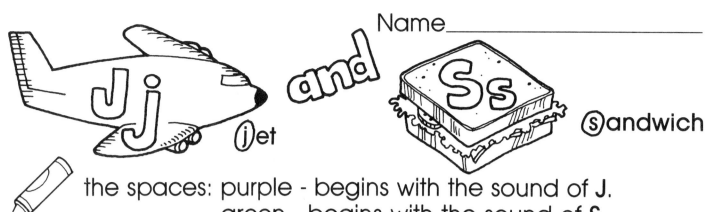

Name_____

Jj and Ss

jet   sandwich

the spaces: purple - begins with the sound of J.
green - begins with the sound of S.

Name_____

Nn or **Ww** under each picture to name its beginning sound.

the pictures: N - blue W - orange

Qq queen and Vv Volcano

the letters. _____ a line from each letter to a picture which begins with the sound of the letter.

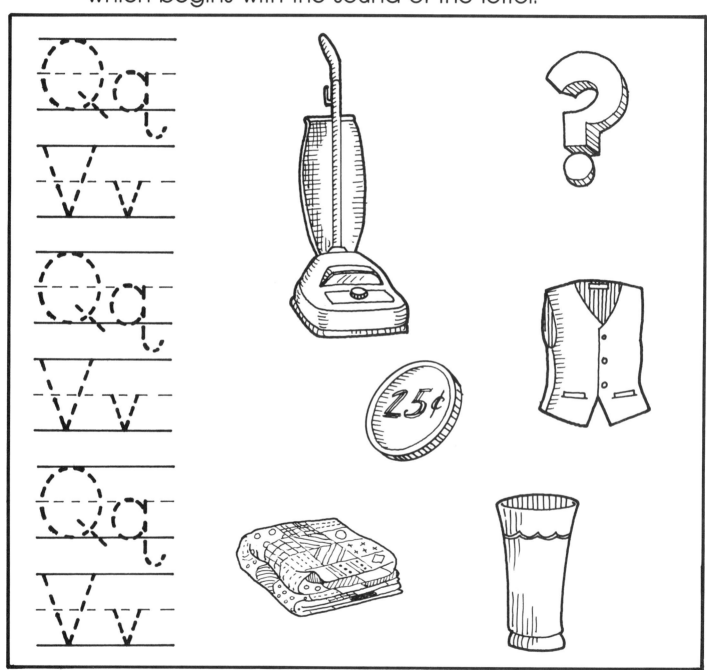

the pictures: Q - yellow   V - red

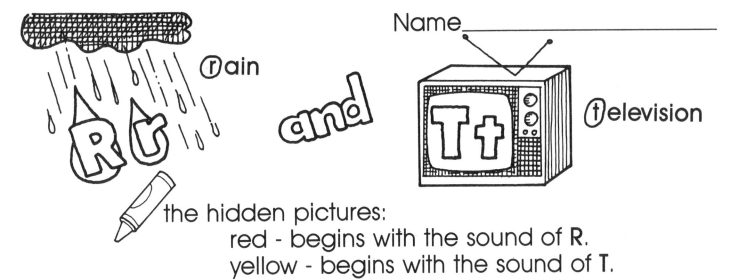

Name_____

ⓡain

and

ⓣelevision

the hidden pictures:
red - begins with the sound of R.
yellow - begins with the sound of T.

Yy Yak and Zz Zoo

the letter that stands for the beginning sound.

y z   y z   y z

y z   y z   y z

y z   y z   y z

the pictures: Y - green   Z - brown

b, f or **d** to name the **ending** sound for each picture.

the pictures: b - red   f - yellow   d - blue

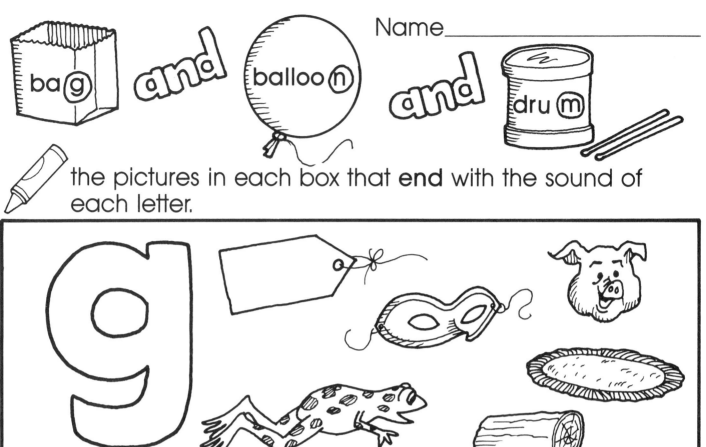

Name_____

the pictures in each box that **end** with the sound of each letter.

 so**a** **p** **and**  ga**s** **and**  boo**k**

a line from each letter to a picture which **ends** with the sound of that letter.

the pictures: **p** - green   **s** - orange   **k** - purple

                                 © 1990 Instructional Fair, Inc.

Name_____

whee**l** and pea**r** and foo**t** and a**x**

✎ the ending sound for each picture.

the pictures: l - red   r - green   t - yellow   x - blue

Begins with... Ends with...

the beginning and ending sound for each picture.

_____ ----- (tag) _____ -----	_____ ----- (mop) _____ -----
_____ ----- (boat) _____ -----	_____ ----- (nail) _____ -----
_____ ----- (sun) _____ -----	_____ ----- (lamp) _____ -----
_____ ----- (gum) _____ -----	_____ ----- (gift) _____ -----
_____ ----- (carrot) _____ -----	_____ ----- (yawn) _____ -----

the pictures.

Begins with...
Ends with...

Name_____

the pictures: yellow - **begins** with the sound of the letter.
purple - **ends** with the sound of the letter.

64

Begins with...
Ends with...

✏ the beginning sound. ✏ a ☐ around the ending sound.

6 — x s b	(can) — c n t	(jeep) — p m j
(rug) — r s g	(foot) — t r f	(top) — b p t
(vest) — t m v	(mug) — k m b	(leaf) — l g f
(sink) — g s k	(ax) — a f x	(doll) — l d v

🖍 the pictures.

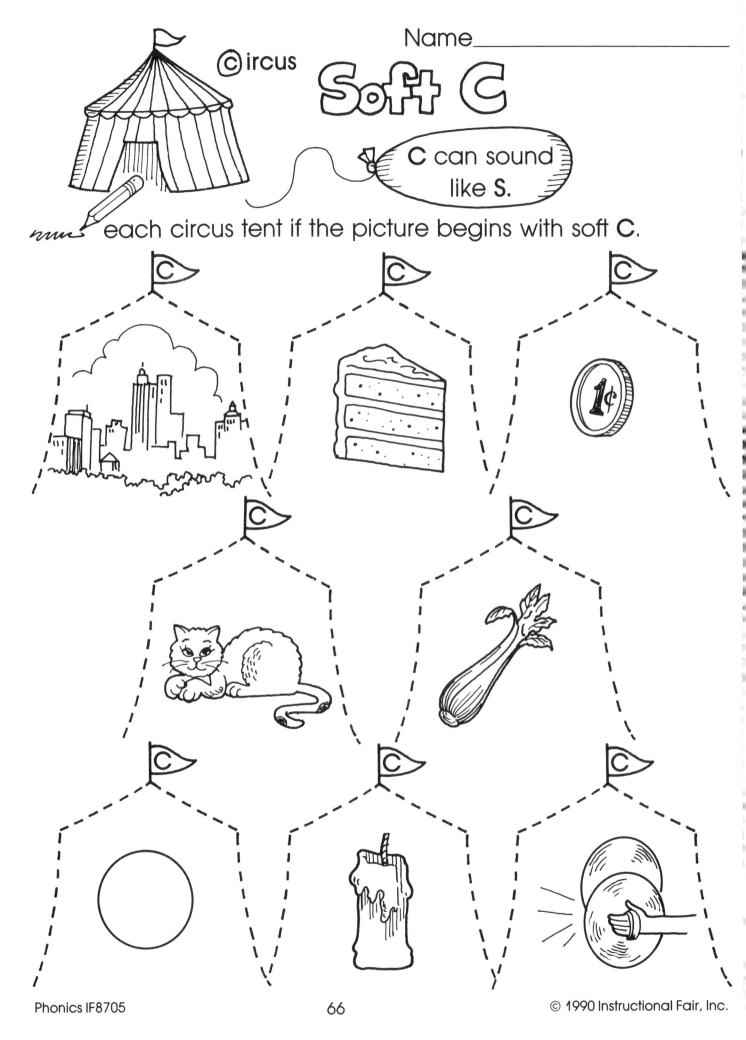

Name_____

Soft C

©ircus

C can sound like S.

✎ each circus tent if the picture begins with soft C.

Short A

Name_____

ă

✎ a on each line. Find the word to match each picture.

✎ each word in the puzzle.

c _ b

m _ sk

_ nt

m _ p

_ x

_ dd

1↓

2→

3→

4↓

5→

6↓

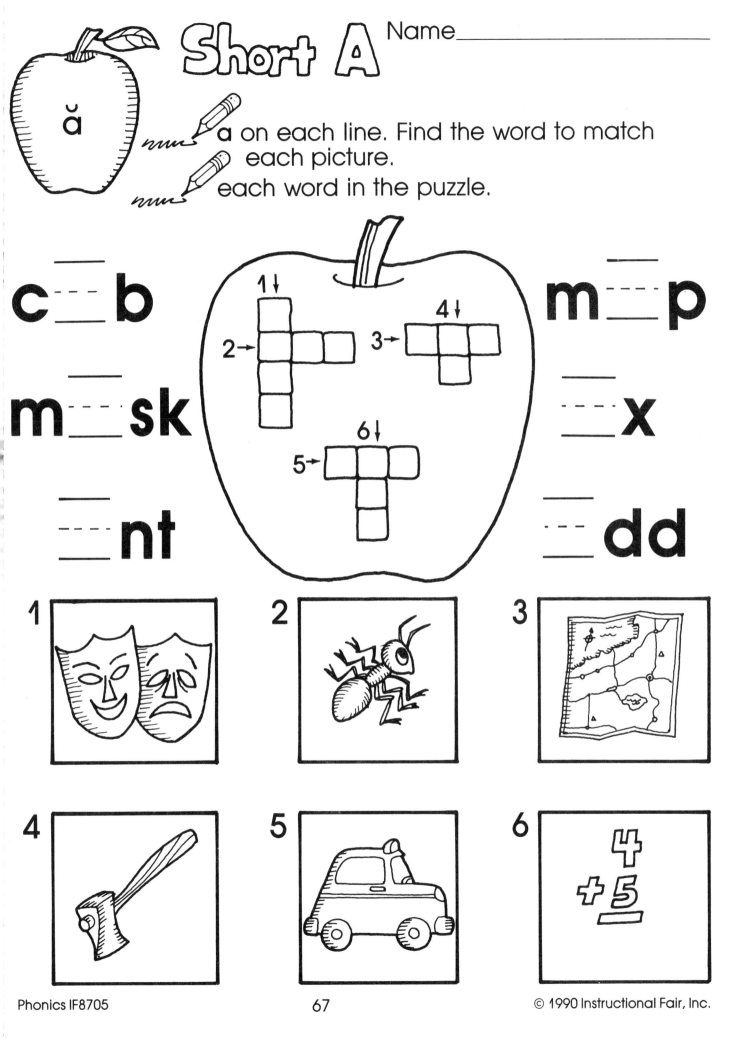

1

2

3

4

5

6
$$\begin{array}{r}4\\+5\\\hline\end{array}$$

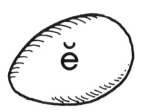

Short E

Unscramble the letters by using the numbers. Write each word. each picture the correct color.

e n t
2 3 1

_____

- - - - - - - - -

_____

blue

t v s e
4 1 3 2

_____

- - - - - - - - -

_____

yellow

w b e
1 3 2

_____

- - - - - - - - -

_____

purple

s d k e
3 1 4 2

_____

- - - - - - - - -

_____

green

l b l e
3 1 4 2

_____

- - - - - - - - -

_____

orange

l e b t
3 2 1 4

_____

- - - - - - - - -

_____

red

Name_____

Short I

Find the correct word for each picture. 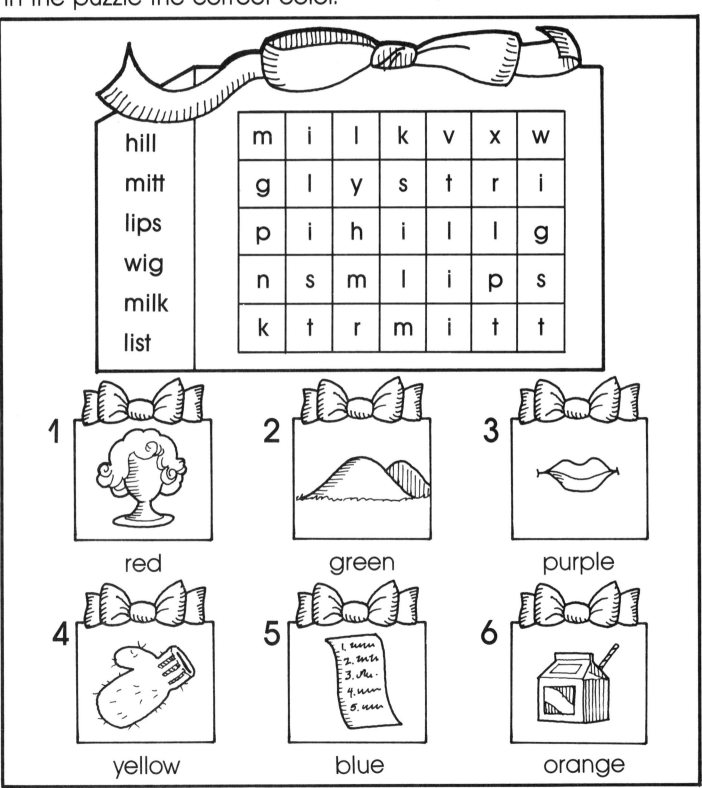 the word squares in the puzzle the correct color.

hill
mitt
lips
wig
milk
list

m	i	l	k	v	x	w
g	l	y	s	t	r	i
p	i	h	i	l	l	g
n	s	m	l	i	p	s
k	t	r	m	i	t	t

1   red

2   green

3   purple

4   yellow

5   blue

6   orange

Name_____

Short O

each ☁ that has two short **O** pictures.

Name_____

Short U

Find the correct word to name each picture. ✏ the correct number in each bubble.

1 - rug 2 - jug 3 - sun 4 - bug
5 - gum 6 - cup 7 - up

the pictures.

Short Vowels

a, e, i, o or u on each line to name the pictures.

_ gg	s _ x	c _ n	_ x
c _ ff	c _ b	l _ g	p _ g
p _ p	h _ m	z _ p	c _ t
h _ n	p _ n	b _ n	f _ n

the pictures: **a** - red **e** - brown **i** - green
o - blue **u** - purple

72 © 1990 Instructional Fair, Inc.

Short Vowels

Name_____

a, e, i, o or u on each line to name each picture.
the correct word in each sentence. the pictures.

f_ _sh   c_ _p   t_ _g

1 - blue
2 - orange
3 - red
4 - purple
5 - green

n_ _st   r_ _ck

_____
- - - - - - - - - - -
1. The _____ is on the gift.

_____
- - - - - - - - - - -
2. The big egg is in the _____.

_____
- - - - - - - - - - -
3. The _____ lives in the pond.

_____
- - - - - - - - - - -
4. The bug sat on the _____.

_____
- - - - - - - - - - -
5. The _____ sits on the dish.

Short Vowels

✏ a, e, i, o or u on each line to name the pictures.

✏ each word in the puzzle:
a - green   e - red   i - yellow   o - blue   u - purple

f _ _ st

l_ _mp

j_ _mp

l	a	m	p	k	j
m	r	i	n	g	u
d	y	r	v	x	m
o	g	n	k	p	p
l	f	i	s	t	b
l	x	d	v	r	m
v	j	e	m	e	n
a	u	s	s	g	y
p	g	k	v	k	t

m_ _n

d_ _ll

r_ _ng   **d_ _ _sk**   **j_ _g**

c@ke

Long A

_____ each picture which has the long sound of A.

_____ the other pictures.

_____ the long A pictures.

Name_____

Long A

the word in each box that names the picture.

the correct word on the lines.

can / cape	rain / ran	get / gate
vet / vase	cane / cap	not / nail
run / rake	mail / met	top / tape
let / lake	cat / cake	cave / cot

the pictures.

Name_____

Long A

 the correct word on each line.  each answer in the puzzle.

rake

mail

cane

tape

s t r m f x r
v a c a n e a
n p b i m s k
g e k l b y e

The man has a _____.

Has the _____ come?

Jane put _____ on the vase.

Dave will get the _____.

Short and Long A

 Put a red **X** on each **short a** picture.
Put a blue ⭕ around each **long a** picture.

NO SWIMMING

lē leaf

Long E

each leaf if the picture has the long sound of **E**.

Long E

e on each line. Draw a line from each word to the correct picture. Color the picture the correct color.

s___al
black

b___e
yellow

p___a
green

b___et
red

h___el
brown

j___ep
blue

Name_____

Long E

Read each sentence. ____ the leaves: **red** - correct word.
                              yellow - other word.

The seal beet has a ball.

Lee has a red pea jeep

Did Bill get his feet bee wet?

Pete has gum on his heel seal

The beet bee is on the gate.

81   © 1990 Instructional Fair, Inc.

Review: Long A and E

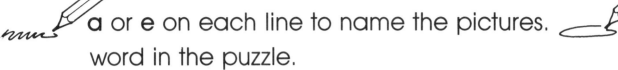

Name _____

___ a or e on each line to name the pictures. ___ each word in the puzzle.

v__se

b__e

s__al

f__et

f	e	e	t	s
x	r	f	k	e
r	a	i	n	a
g	k	v	b	l
m	e	p	e	v
c	a	p	e	a
r	x	v	c	s
b	e	e	t	e

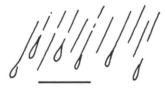

r__in

c__pe

r__ke

b__et

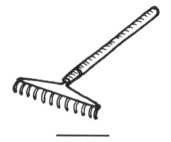

___ the pictures: **long a - red**   **long e - green**

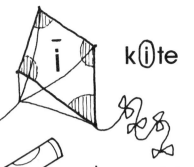

kite

Long I

each space yellow if the picture has the long sound of I.

Name_____

Long I

i on each line. Color each kite the correct color.

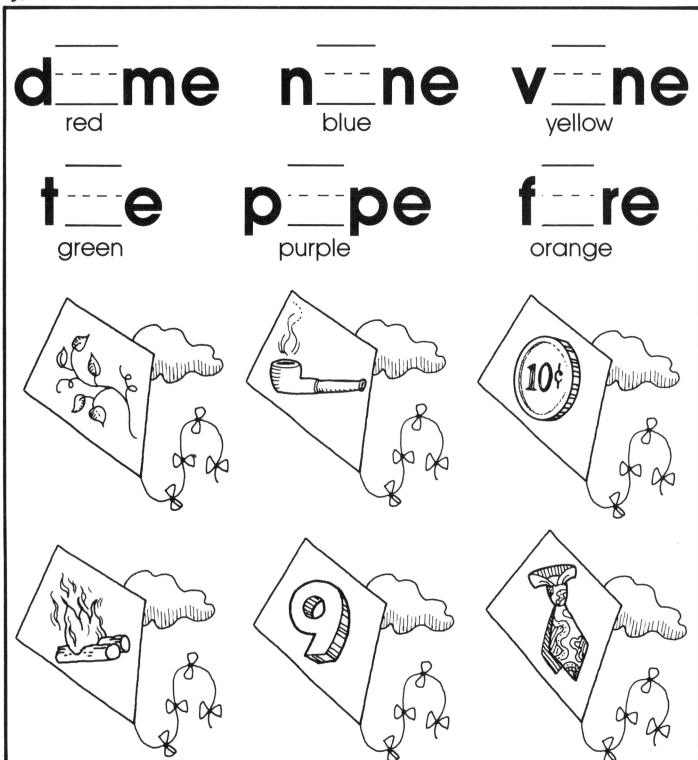

d__me
red

n__ne
blue

v__ne
yellow

t__e
green

p__pe
purple

f__re
orange

Name_____

Long I

✏ the correct word on each line. 🖍 each picture the correct color.

1.
tie
fire

red
_____
- - - - - - - - -
Mike put a log on the _____.

2.
ice
nine

blue
_____
- - - - - - - - -
The sun will melt the _____.

3.
bike
dime

green
_____
- - - - - - - - -
The apple costs a _____.

4.
hive
pipe

brown
_____
- - - - - - - - -
The bee is in the _____.

1.   2.   3. 10¢ EACH   4.

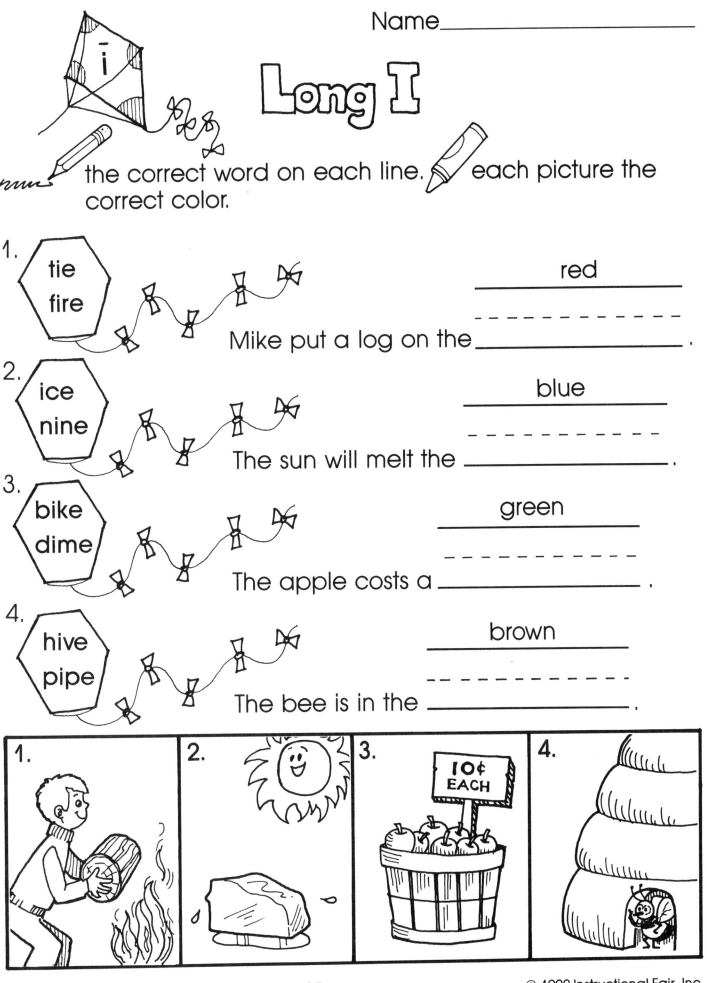

Short and Long I

a blue ◯ around each **short** I picture.

an orange **X** on each **long** I picture.

86

Review: Long A E I

Say the name of each picture. ✏ a, e or i in each ☐ to name the long vowel that you hear.

☐ cheese	☐ tie	☐ skate	☐ 5
☐ chain	☐ queen	☐ slide	☐ nail
☐ 3	☐ bride	☐ cave	☐ jeep
☐ whistle	☐ beans	☐ knife	☐ hive

✏ the pictures: a - green   e - orange   i - purple

Name_____

Long O

c⊙ne

the cones: blue - if the picture has the long sound of O.
orange - other cones.

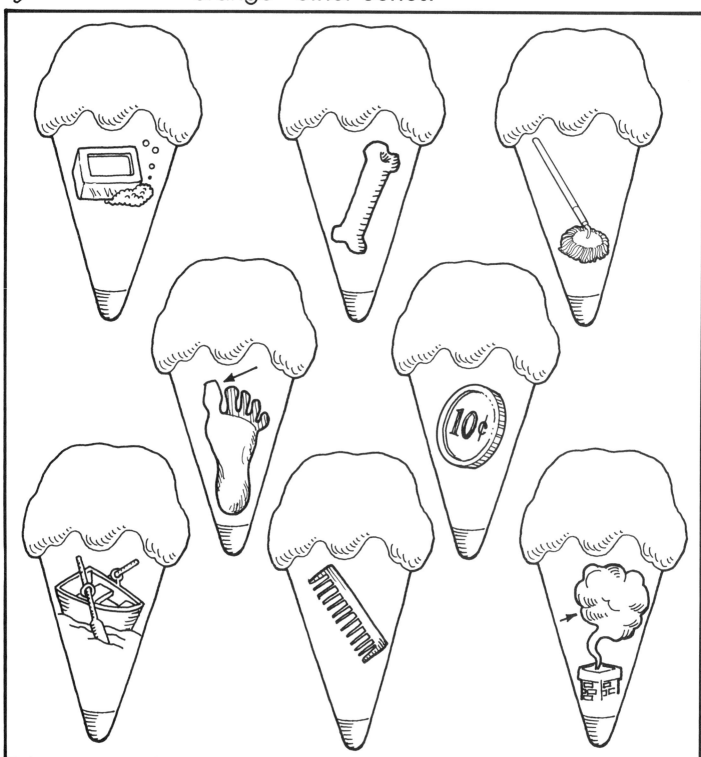

Long O

o on each line. the correct picture for each word.

r__pe	g__at
n__se	h__e
r__se	s__ap
b__ne	r__be

Long O

the correct word on each line. each answer in the puzzle.

robe

bone

boat

nose

1. The bee sat on his _____.

2. Bo gave his dog a _____.

3. Rose likes to ride in the _____.

4. Joe has an old red _____.

Short and Long O

the pictures: **short o** - red
long o - yellow

91

Review: Long A E I O

a, e, i or o on each line to name the pictures.

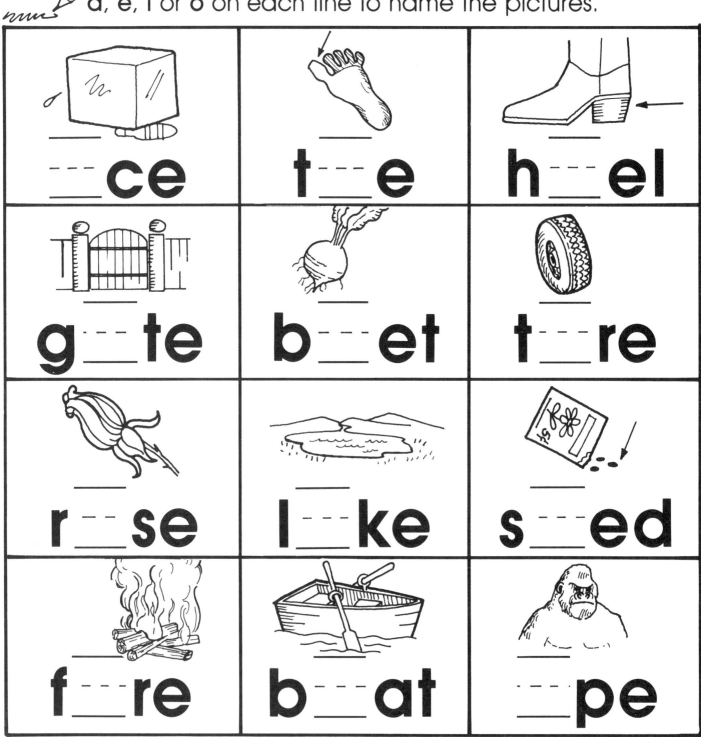

_ _ ce   t _ e   h _ _ el

g _ _ te   b _ _ et   t _ _ re

r _ _ se   l _ ke   s _ _ ed

f _ re   b _ _ at   _ _ pe

the pictures: a - yellow   e - blue   i - green   o - orange

Name_____

Long U

u on each line. ✏ the picture for each word with the correct color.

1
f__se

2
t__ne

3
s__it

4
j__ice

5
c__be

6
m__le

1 - red
2 - blue
3 - yellow
4 - green
5 - purple
6 - orange

Long U

Name_____

the correct word for each sentence. the word on the line.

	The mule sips the _____ .	tune juice
	The mule lit the _____ .	fuse suit
	The mule has a cute _____ .	cube suit
	The mule licks the ice _____ .	tube cube
	The mule likes the _____ .	tune juice

Short and Long U

a green **X** on each **short u** picture.

a purple ◯ around each **long u** picture.

95

Review: Long

Ā E I O U

the pictures in each row with the correct vowel sound.

ā				
ē				
ī				
ō				
ū				

Review: Long

A E I O U

the hidden pictures:

a - yellow   **e** - red   **i** - green   **o** - purple   **u** - blue

Name_____

Short and Long a e i o u

the correct pictures in each box.

ă - blue ā - orange	   
ĕ - red ē - yellow	   
ĭ - green ī - purple	 
ŏ - yellow ō - blue	   
ŭ - green ū - orange	   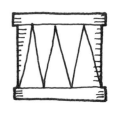

Short and Long a e i o u

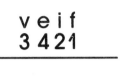 the letters on each line in the correct order.

_____ a line to match each word and picture.

the pictures: **short vowel** - purple **long vowel** - green

v e i f
3 4 2 1

_____

- - - - - - - -

k d s e
4 1 3 2

_____

- - - - - - - -

o p a s
2 4 3 1

_____

- - - - - - - -

s m k a
3 1 4 2

_____

- - - - - - - -

u l m e
2 3 1 4

_____

- - - - - - - -

Short and Long a e i o u

Name_____

✏ _ a, e, i, o or u on each line to name the pictures.

🖍 _ the pictures: short vowel - red   long vowel - blue

d_ck	p_il	k_te	l_mp
p_as	c_be	b_x	b_lt
l_st	c_ne	b_g	r_ke
t_ne	s_al	d_ll	t_re

Short and Long a e i o u

Name_____

the parts of each kite which have the correct vowel sound.

jet
tent
deep
bed

up
mule
cute
tune

cape
rain
tape
can

pipe bike
bib ice

pop
cot
rope
fox

ă

ĕ

ī

ŏ

ū

101

© 1990 Instructional Fair, Inc.

Short and Long a e i o u

 the hidden pictures: **short vowels** - green
long vowels - yellow

Today's Special

102

Answer Key

Page 4

103

© 1990 Instructional Fair, Inc.

Answer Key

Name

S S S s s s

a line from the sun to each picture which begins with the sound of S.

the S pictures.

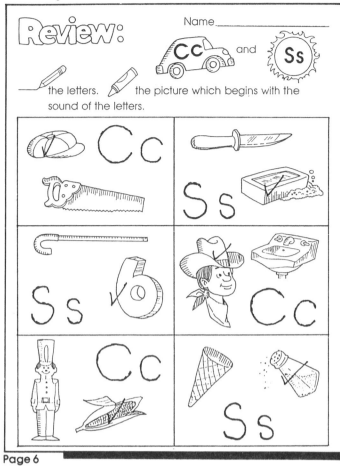

Review:

Cc and Ss

Name

the letters. the picture which begins with the sound of the letters.

dog

Name

D D D d d d

the letters. the pictures in each row which begin with the sound of D.

the D pictures.

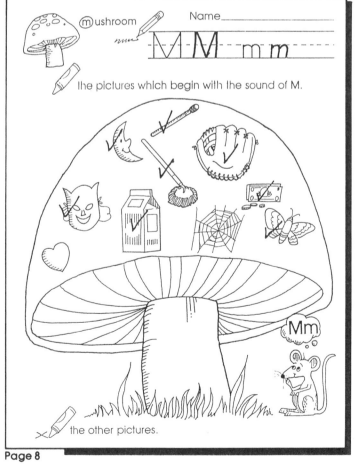

mushroom

Name

M M m m

the pictures which begin with the sound of M.

Mm

the other pictures.

Answer Key

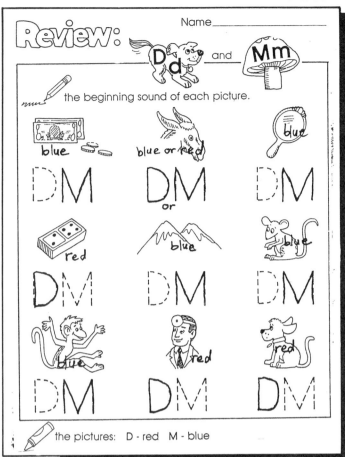

Review: Dd and Mm

_____ the beginning sound of each picture.

blue

blue or red

blue

DM   DM _or_   DM

red

blue

DM   DM   DM

blue

red

red

DM   DM   DM

_____ the pictures: D - red   M - blue

Page 9

ⓕish

F F F   f f f

_____ each picture which begins with the sound of F.

✓   ✓   ✓

✗   ✓   ✓

✓   ✗   ✓

✓   ✗   ✓

✗ _____ the other pictures.

Page 10

ⓡainbow

R R R   r r r

_____ a line from the Rr to each picture which begins with the sound of R.

R r

_____ the R pictures.

Page 11

Review: Ff and Rr

_____ the letters. _____ a line from each letter to a picture which begins with the sound of the letter.

F f
R r
F f
R r
F f
R r
F f

_____ the pictures: F - purple   R - green

Page 12

Answer Key

Gg under each picture which begins with the sound of G.

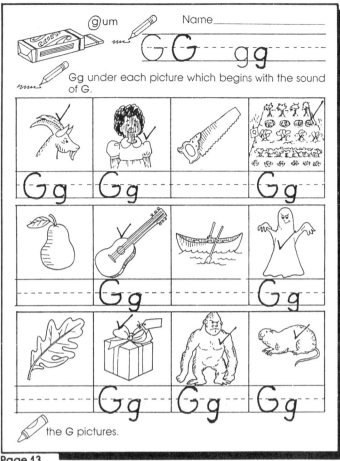

the G pictures.

Page 13

---

the picture in each ⬦ that begins with the sound of P.

the other pictures.

Page 14

Review: Gg and Pp

the picture which begins with the sound of each letter.

Page 15

---

a line from the web to each picture which begins with the sound of W.

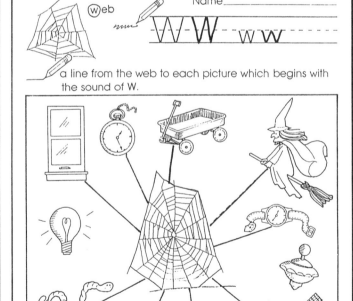

the W pictures.

Page 16

Answer Key

jam

Trace the letters. Circle the pictures in each row which begin with the sound of J.

Color the J pictures.

Review: Ww and Jj

Circle the letter that stands for the beginning sound of each picture.

Color the pictures: W - yellow   J - red

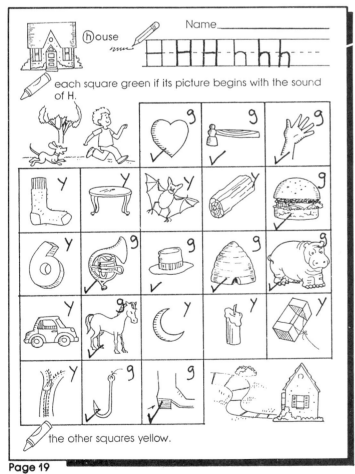

house

Color each square green if its picture begins with the sound of H.

Color the other squares yellow.

nest

Trace. Draw a line from each nest to a picture which begins with the sound of N.

Color the N pictures.

Answer Key

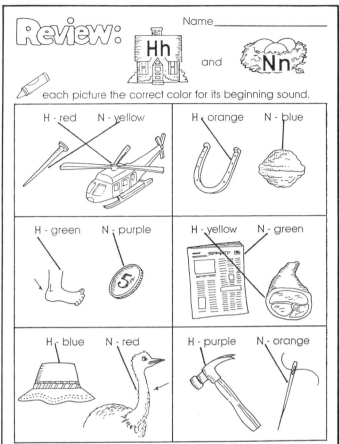

Page 21

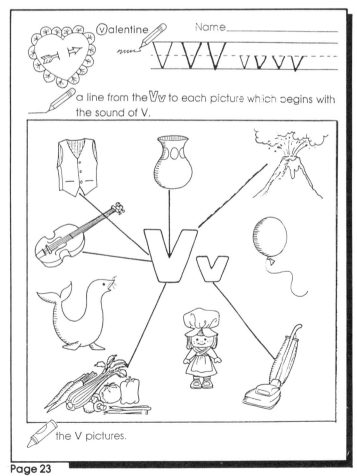

Page 23

Page 24

Answer Key

Page 25

Page 26

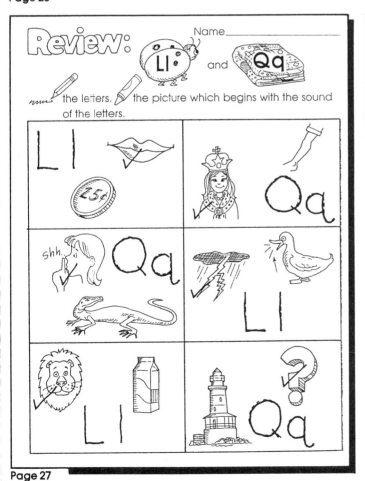

Page 27

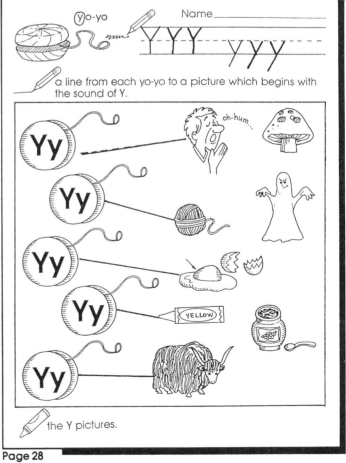

Page 28

© 1990 Instructional Fair, Inc.

Answer Key

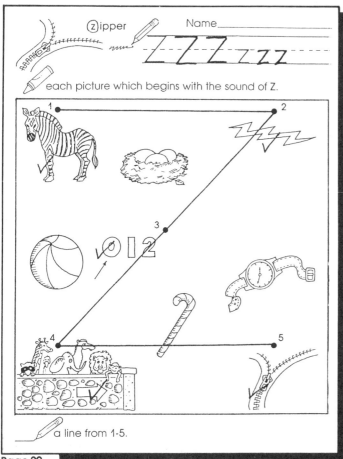

Page 29

Page 30

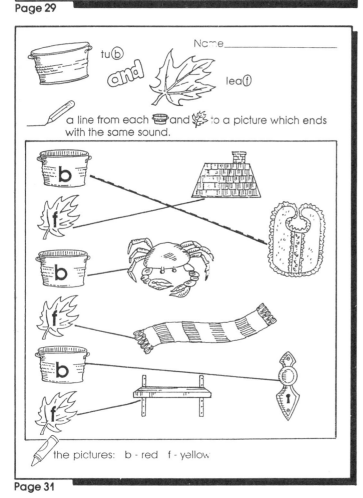

Page 31

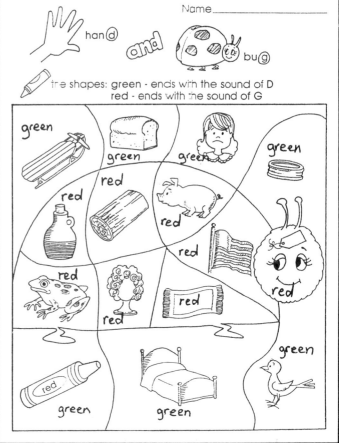

Page 32

Answer Key

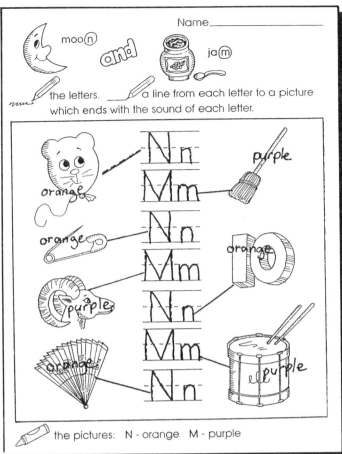

Page 33

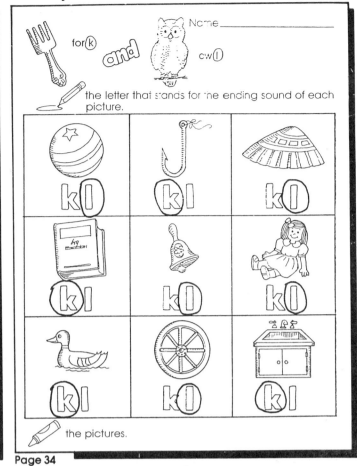

Page 34

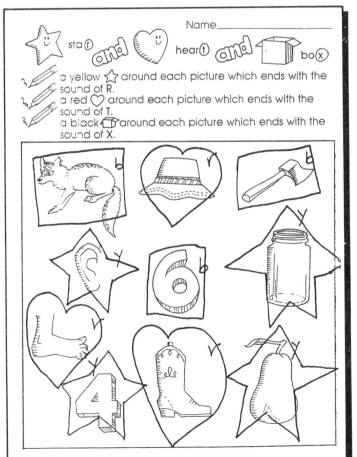

Page 35

Page 36

Answer Key

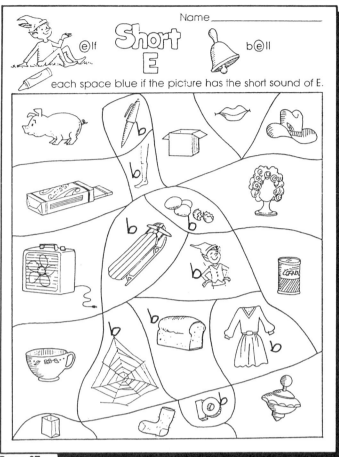

Short E

elf   b(e)ll

color each space blue if the picture has the short sound of E.

Page 37

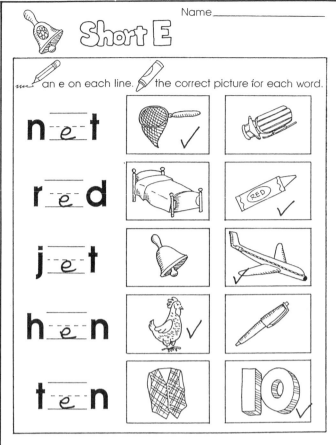

Short E

Write an e on each line. Color the correct picture for each word.

n e t

r e d

j e t

h e n

t e n

Page 38

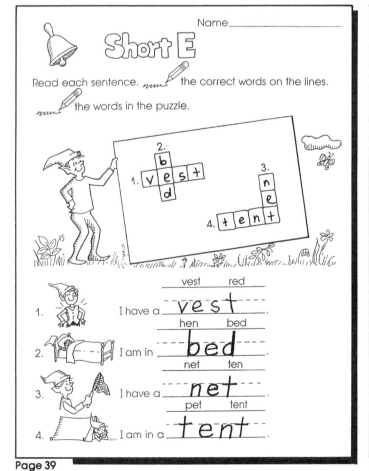

Short E

Read each sentence. Write the correct words on the lines.
Color the words in the puzzle.

2. b
1. v e s t
d
3. n
e
4. t e n t

vest   red
1. I have a   vest

hen   bed
2. I am in   bed

net   ten
3. I have a   net

pet   tent
4. I am in a   tent

Page 39

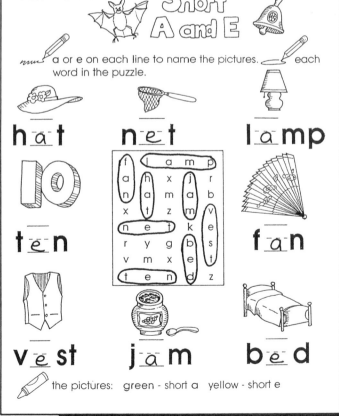

Review: Short A and E

Write a or e on each line to name the pictures. Color each
word in the puzzle.

h a t   n e t   l a mp

10

t e n   f a n

v e st   j a m   b e d

Color the pictures: green - short a   yellow - short e

Page 40

Answer Key

Name_____

Short I

i on each line. the correct picture for each word.

p i g	l i d
s i x	m i lk
w i g	p i n
g i ft	l i ps

Page 41

Review: Short I

Name_____

Read each sentence. the correct words on the lines.
the words in the puzzle.

bib	pig

I have a **bib**

six	wig

I have a **wig**

list	pin

I have a **list**

mitt	lid

I have a **mitt**

Page 42

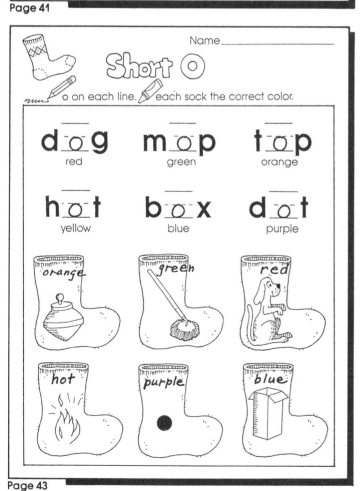

Name_____

Short O

o on each line. each sock the correct color.

d o g	m o p	t o p
red	green	orange
h o t	b o x	d o t
yellow	blue	purple

orange green red

hot purple blue

Page 43

Name_____

Short O

Read each sentence. the correct word. the word on the line.

I have a **sock**	(sock) cot
I have a **doll**	hot (doll)
I have a **job**	(job) mop
I have a **rod**	(rod) fox
I have a **pot**	dot (pot)

Page 44

Phonics IF8705

113

© 1990 Instructional Fair, Inc.

Answer Key

Short U

ⓤp   d(u)ck

each space purple if the picture has the short sound of U.

(spaces marked with y and p)

the other spaces yellow.

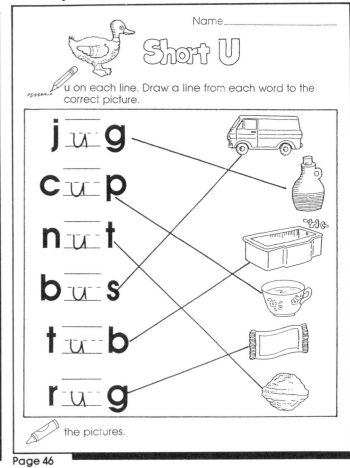

Short U

u on each line. Draw a line from each word to the correct picture.

j **u** g
c **u** p
n **u** t
b **u** s
t **u** b
r **u** g

the pictures.

Short U

Read each sentence. ▢ the correct ▭ to match the picture.

duck

1. The duck has a   cup ✓ | tub
2. The duck has a   jug | nut ✓
3. The duck has a   gum | bus ✓
4. The duck has a   bug ✓ | sun
5. The duck has a   tub | rug ✓

the pictures.

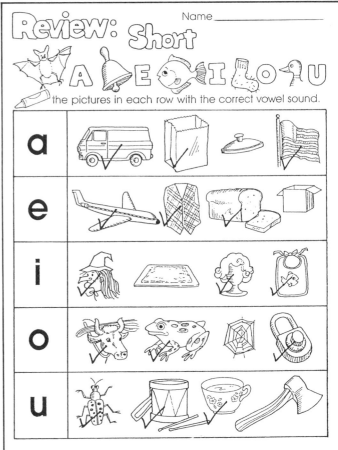

Review: Short

A E I O U

the pictures in each row with the correct vowel sound.

a
e
i
o
u

Answer Key

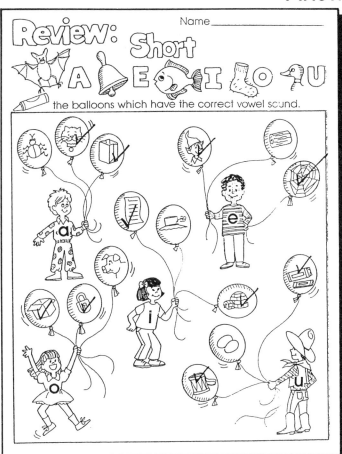

Review: Short A E I O U

the balloons which have the correct vowel sound.

Page 49

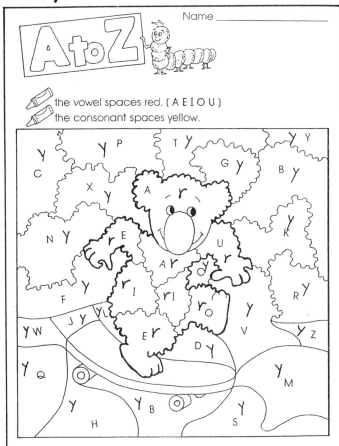

A to Z

the vowel spaces red. (A E I O U)
the consonant spaces yellow.

Page 50

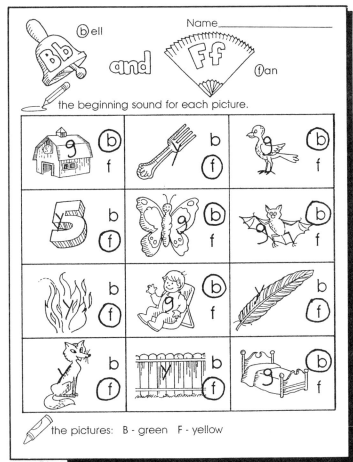

Bb bell **and** **Ff** fan

the beginning sound for each picture.

the pictures: B - green   F - yellow

Page 51

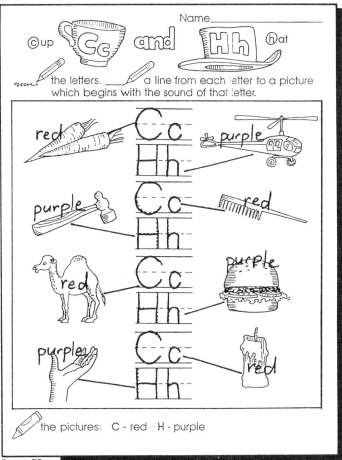

cup **Cc** **and** **Hh** **h**at

the letters. _____ a line from each letter to a picture which begins with the sound of that letter.

red	purple
purple	red
red	purple
purple	red

the pictures: C - red   H - purple

Page 52

Phonics IF8705

115

© 1990 Instructional Fair, Inc.

Answer Key

Name_____

Gg gift and **Mm** mitten

the beginning sound of each picture.

the pictures: G - brown   M - red

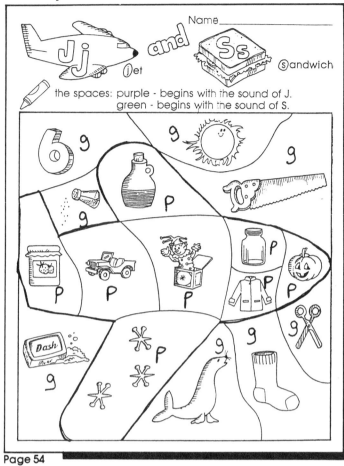

Name_____

Jj jet and **Ss** sandwich

the spaces: purple - begins with the sound of J.
green - begins with the sound of S.

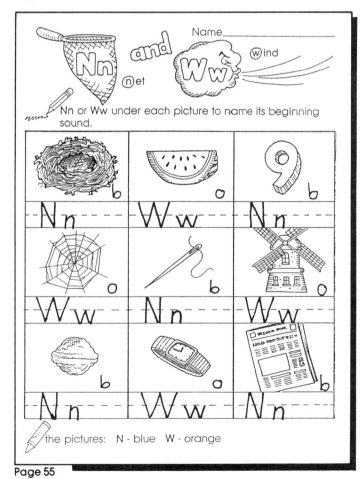

Name_____

Nn net and **Ww** wind

Nn or Ww under each picture to name its beginning
sound.

the pictures: N - blue   W - orange

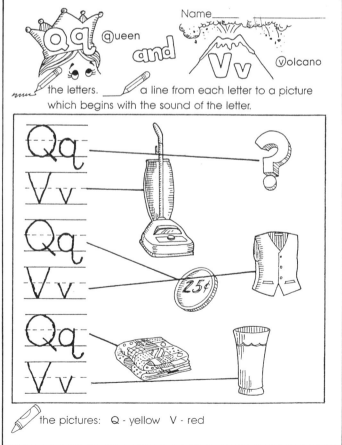

Name_____

Qq queen and **Vv** volcano

the letters. a line from each letter to a picture
which begins with the sound of the letter.

the pictures: Q - yellow   V - red

© 1990 Instructional Fair, Inc.

Answer Key

Page 57

Name_____

(r)ain   and   (t)elevision

the hidden pictures:
red - begins with the sound of R.
yellow - begins with the sound of T.

Page 57

Page 58

Name_____

(Y)ak   and   (z)oo

the letter that stands for the beginning sound.

the pictures: Y - green Z - brown

Page 58

Page 59

Name_____

tu(b)   and   roo(f)   and   brea(d)

b, f or d to name the ending sound for each picture.

red	blue	yellow	red
b	d	d	b
yellow	blue	yellow	blue
f	f	f	d
red	yellow	blue	red
f	f	f	d

the pictures: b - red f - yellow d - blue

Page 59

Page 60

Name_____

ba(g)   and   balloo(n)   and   dru(m)

the pictures in each box that end with the sound of each letter.

Page 60

Phonics IF8705   117   © 1990 Instructional Fair, Inc.

Answer Key

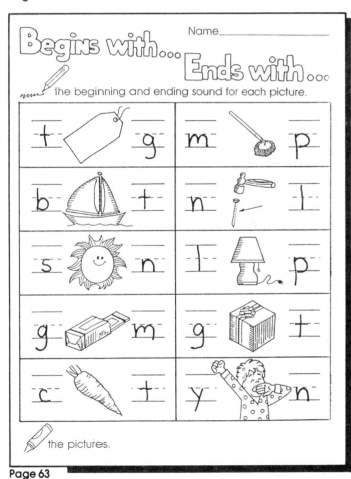

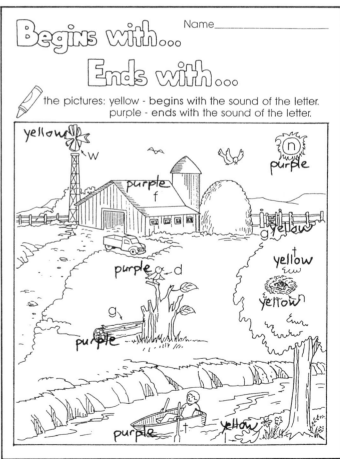

118

© 1990 Instructional Fair, Inc.

Answer Key

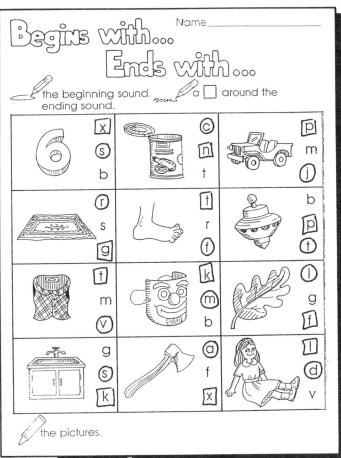

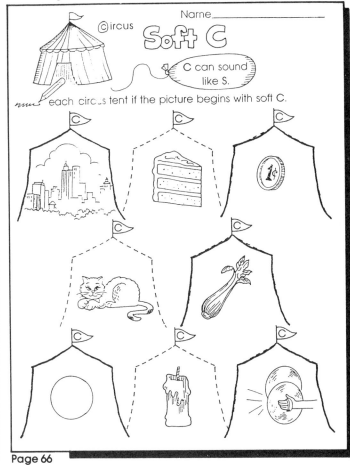

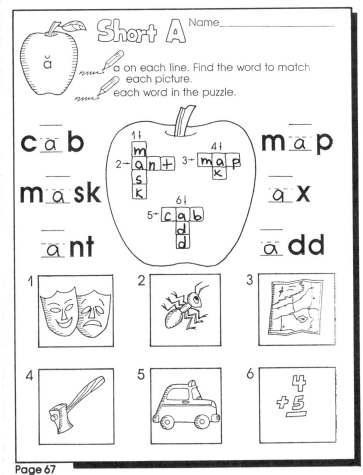

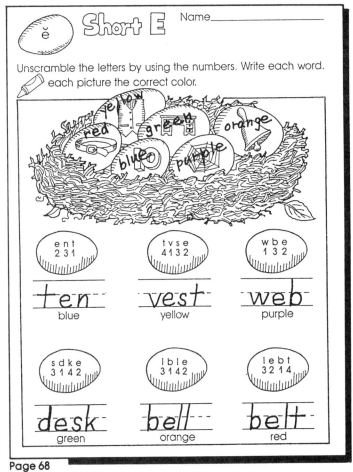

Page 65

Page 66

Page 67

Page 68

Phonics IF8705

119

© 1990 Instructional Fair, Inc.

Answer Key

Short I

Name_____

Find the correct word for each picture. [crayon] the word squares in the puzzle the correct color.

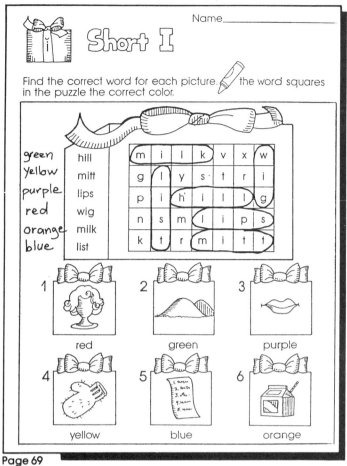

green — hill
yellow — mitt
purple — lips
red — wig
orange — milk
blue — list

1 red
2 green
3 purple
4 yellow
5 blue
6 orange

Short O

Name_____

[crayon] each ⬭ that has two short O pictures.

Short U

Name_____

Find the correct word to name each picture. [pencil] the correct number in each bubble.

1 - rug 2 - jug 3 - sun 4 - bug
5 - gum 6 - cup 7 - up

[crayon] the pictures.

Short Vowels

Name_____

[pencil] a, e, i, o or u on each line to name the pictures.

brown	green	red	blue
e g g	s i x	c a n	o x
purple red	brown		green
c u f f	c a b	l e g	p i g
blue	red	green	blue
p o p	h a m	z i p	c o t
brown	green	purple	red
h e n	p i n	b u n	f a n

[crayon] the pictures: a - red e - brown i - green
o - blue u - purple

Answer Key

Short Vowels

a, e, i, o or u on each line to name each picture.
the correct word in each sentence.
the pictures.

f**i**sh   c**u**p   t**a**g

1 - blue
2 - orange
3 - red
4 - purple
5 - green

n**e**st   r**o**ck

1. The ___tag___ is on the gift.

2. The big egg is in the ___nest___

3. The ___fish___ lives in the pond.

4. The bug sat on the ___rock___

5. The ___cup___ sits on the dish.

Short Vowels

a, e, i, o or u on each line to name the pictures.
each word in the puzzle:
a - green   e - red   i - yellow   o - blue   u - purple

f**i**st

l**a**mp   j**u**mp

m**e**n   d**o**ll

r**i**ng   d**e**sk   j**u**g

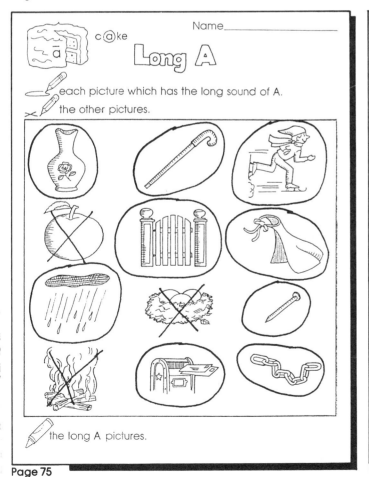

c**a**ke

Long A

each picture which has the long sound of A.
the other pictures.

the long A pictures.

ā

Long A

the word in each box that names the picture.
the correct word on the lines.

can / **cape**	**rain** / ran	get / **gate**
cape	rain	gate
vet / **vase**	**cane** / cap	not / **nail**
vase	cane	nail
run / **rake**	**mail** / met	top / **tape**
rake	mail	tape
let / **lake**	cat / **cake**	**cave** / cot
lake	cake	cave

the pictures.

Long A

Name_____

✎ the correct word on each line. ✐ each answer in the puzzle.

rake
mail
cane
tape

The man has a __cane__.

Has the __mail__ come?

Jane put __tape__ on the vase.

Dave will get the __rake__.

Page 77

Short and Long A

Name_____

🖍 Put a red X on each short a picture.
Put a blue ◯ around each long a picture.

Answers may vary.

Page 78

Long E

Name_____

l e af

🖍 each leaf if the picture has the long sound of E.

Page 79

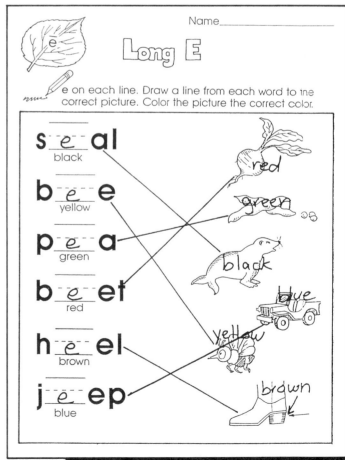

Long E

Name_____

✏ e on each line. Draw a line from each word to the correct picture. Color the picture the correct color.

s e al
black

b e e
yellow

p e a
green

b e et
red

h e el
brown

j e ep
blue

red
green
black
blue
yellow
brown

Page 80

Answer Key

Long E

Read each sentence. ✓ the leaves: red - correct word.
yellow - other word.

The ~~seal~~ **beet** has a ball.

Lee has a red **pea** ~~jeep~~.

Did Bill get his ~~feet~~ **bee** wet?

Pete has gum on his ~~heel~~ **seal**.

The ~~beet~~ **bee** is on the gate.

Page 81

Review: Long A and E

a or e on each line to name the pictures. ✓ each
word in the puzzle.

red — v a se

green — f ee t

red — c a pe

green — b ee

red — r a ke

green — b ee t

f	e	e	t	s
x	r	f	k	e
r	a	i	n	a
g	k	v	b	l
m	e	p	e	v
c	a	p	e	a
r	x	v	c	s
b	e	e	t	e

green — s e al

red — r a in

green — b ee t

the pictures: long a - red   long e - green

Page 82

Long I

kite

each space yellow if the picture has the long sound of I.

yellow, yellow, yellow, yellow, yellow, yellow, yellow, yellow

Page 83

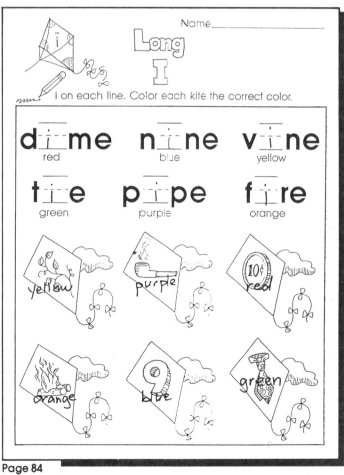

Long I

kite

i on each line. Color each kite the correct color.

d i me
red

n i ne
blue

v i ne
yellow

t i e
green

p i pe
purple

f i re
orange

yellow   purple   red

orange   blue   green

Page 84

Answer Key

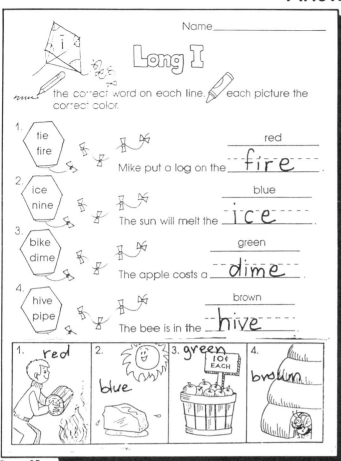

Long I

Name_____

the correct word on each line. each picture the correct color.

1. tie / fire — red — Mike put a log on the **fire**
2. ice / nine — blue — The sun will melt the **ice**
3. bike / dime — green — The apple costs a **dime**
4. hive / pipe — brown — The bee is in the **hive**

1. red 2. blue 3. green 10¢ EACH 4. brown

Page 85

Short and Long I

Name_____

a blue ○ around each short I picture.
an orange X on each long I picture.

Answers may vary.

Grandma's

Page 86

Review: Long A E I

Name_____

Say the name of each picture. a, e or i in each □ to name the long vowel that you hear.

e orange	i purple	a green	i purple 5
a green	e orange	i purple	a green
e orange 3	i purple	a green	e orange
a green	e orange	I knife	i purple

the pictures: a - green e - orange i - purple

Page 87

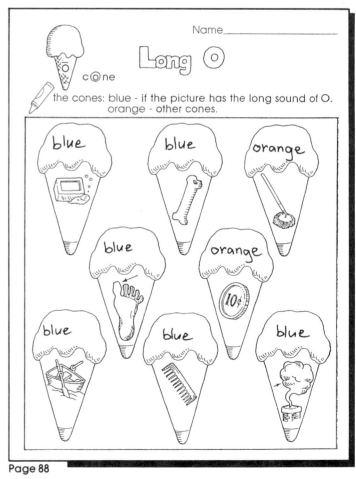

Long O

Name_____

c○ne

the cones: blue - if the picture has the long sound of O.
orange - other cones.

blue   blue   orange
blue   orange
blue   blue   blue

Page 88

Answer Key

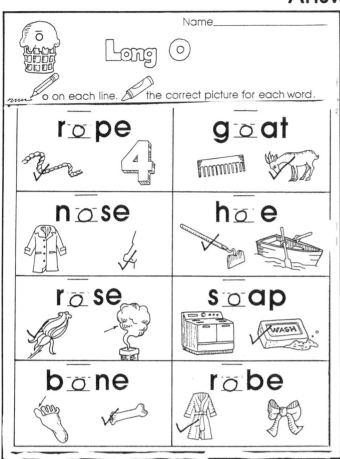

Long O

___ o on each line. ✏ the correct picture for each word.

r**o**pe 4	g**o**at
n**o**se	h**o**e
r**o**se	s**o**ap
b**o**ne	r**o**be

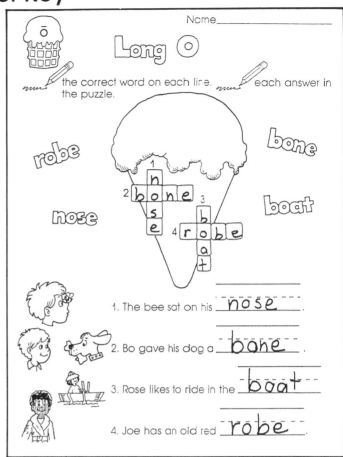

Long O

___ the correct word on each line. ___ each answer in the puzzle.

robe   bone

nose   boat

1. The bee sat on his **nose**

2. Bo gave his dog a **bone**.

3. Rose likes to ride in the **boat**

4. Joe has an old red **robe**.

Short and Long O

✏ the pictures: short o - red
long o - yellow **Answers may vary.**

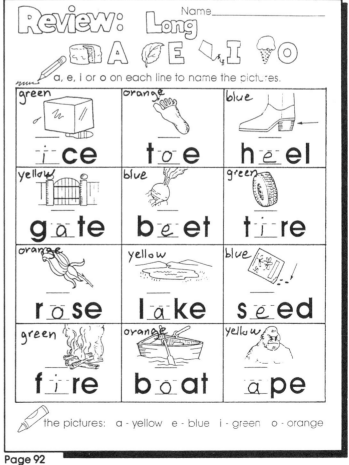

Review: Long A E I O

✏ a, e, i or o on each line to name the pictures.

green	orange	blue
ice	t**o**e	h**e**el
yellow	blue	green
g**a**te	b**e**et	t**i**re
orange	yellow	blue
r**o**se	l**a**ke	s**ee**d
green	orange	yellow
f**i**re	b**o**at	**a**pe

✏ the pictures: a - yellow   e - blue   i - green   o - orange

Answer Key

Page 93

Long U

u on each line. the picture for each word with the correct color.

1	2	3
f u se	t u ne	su i t

4	5	6
ju i ce	c u be	m u le

green
red
blue
orange
purple
yellow

1 - red
2 - blue
3 - yellow
4 - green
5 - purple
6 - orange

Page 94

Long U

the correct word for each sentence. the word on the line.

	The mule sips the _juice_	tune / (juice)
	The mule lit the _fuse_	(fuse) / suit
	The mule has a cute _suit_	cube / (suit)
	The mule licks the ice _cube_	tube / (cube)
	The mule likes the _tune_	(tune) / juice

Page 95

Short and Long U

a green X on each short u picture.
a purple ○ around each long u picture.

Answers may vary.

MUSIC SHOP (drum)

(up)

BUS STOP

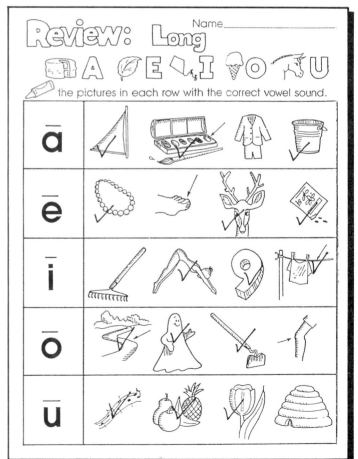

Page 96

Review: Long A E I O U

the pictures in each row with the correct vowel sound.

ā				
ē				
ī				
ō				
ū				

Answer Key

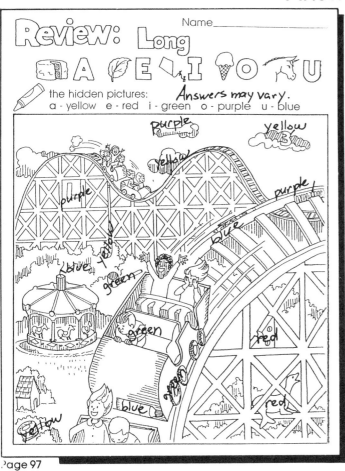

Review: Long A E I O U

🖍 the hidden pictures: *Answers may vary.*
a - yellow   e - red   i - green   o - purple   u - blue

Short and Long a e i o u

🖍 the correct pictures in each box.

🖍 ă - blue / ā - orange	blue	blue	orange
🖍 ĕ - red / ē - yellow	red	yellow	red	yellow
🖍 ĭ - green / ī - purple	purple	green	green
🖍 ŏ - yellow / ō - blue	yellow	blue	yellow	blue
🖍 ŭ - green / ū - orange	orange	green	orange	green

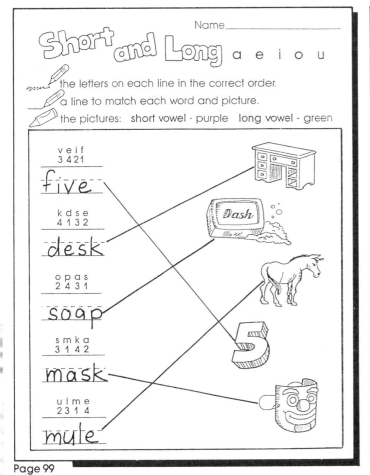

Short and Long a e i o u

✏ the letters on each line in the correct order.
🖍 a line to match each word and picture.
🖍 the pictures: short vowel - purple   long vowel - green

veif
3 4 2 1
five

kdse
4 1 3 2
desk

opas
2 4 3 1
soap

smka
3 1 4 2
mask

ulme
2 3 1 4
mute

Short and Long a e i o u

✏ a, e, i, o or u on each line to name the pictures.
🖍 the pictures: short vowel - red   long vowel - blue

red	blue	blue	red
duck	**pail**	**kite**	**lamp**
blue	blue	red	red
peas	**cube**	**box**	**belt**
red	blue	red	blue
list	**cone**	**bug**	**rake**
blue	blue	red	blue
tune	**seal**	**doll**	**tire**

Answer Key

Page 101

Page 102

About the book . . .

The activities in this book cover a large selection of phonics skills with a sequenced approach and illustrations that enhance motivation. They can be used to provide the foundation of a complete and extensive phonics program. Yet, each skill is addressed in an independent nature to allow for easy coordination with any basal text's approach. The skills addressed are: alphabet recognition, beginning consonant sounds, ending consonant sounds, short vowels, long vowels, and vowel discrimination.

About the author . . .

Holly Fitzgerald's special expertise in all areas of Language Arts has been gained through over fifteen years of varied teaching experiences at the elementary level. She also holds a Master's Degree in Education from Vanderbilt University.

Author: Holly Fitzgerald
Editor: Lee Quackenbush
Artist: Pat Biggs
Cover Art: Jan Vonk